CW00736214

FR⌐

1 3 1789040 1

The Cultural Marxist Assault on Western Civilization

DANIEL JUPP

ISBN (Print Edition): 978-1-54398-203-9
ISBN (eBook Edition): 978-1-54398-204-6

Contents

"A nation can survive its fools, and even the ambitious. But it cannot survive treason from within. An enemy at the gates is less formidable, for he is known and carries his banner openly. But the traitor moves amongst those within the gate freely, his sly whispers rustling through all the alleys, heard in the very halls of government itself."

Cicero

"I have learned to hate all traitors, and there is no disease that I spit on more than treachery."

Aeschylus

"I know not what treason is, if sapping and betraying the liberties of a people is not treason."

Cato the Younger

"Liberals have a preternatural gift for striking a position on the side of treason... Whenever the nation is under attack, from within or without, the liberals side with the enemy."

Ann Coulter

Book One

The Heritage of the West

"The heart of a father is the masterpiece of nature."

—Antoine François Prévost, *Manon Lescaut*

In recent years, like millions of other ordinary people in the highly developed nations of the West, I have discovered to my surprise that, according to some, I am an extremist. I have always been a fairly mild conservative, in my own eyes. I believe in classical liberal values like freedom of speech and religion, the separation of Church and State, a civilised standard of human rights, but also in things like patriotism and a love of the history and culture of my own nation. These seem like fairly moderate and sensible things to me. My father was a Conservative voter of the struggling lower middle class. His father was a postman, and my mother's father was a fishmonger. Both sides of my family were South Londoners, but by the time I was thinking about such things my parents had long since moved out of the city to live in various different parts of Essex. One grandfather continued to live in the leafier suburbs of outer London, and we would travel back every Christmas for a huge family dinner. Other aunts and uncles lived in places like Croydon and Anerley, although over time, like us, more and more of them moved away.

My father loved the British countryside and I don't think he objected to moving out of the city at all. Every time we moved, it seemed to be towards a smaller village more deeply nestled in a patchwork of fields. I was never conscious of being especially poor when I was a child, and except by relative standards I wasn't. My parents spent quite a bit on us at Christmas and my father rose to various middle management positions with different companies. Neither of my parents ever shared money worries with us or stinted in any way, and it was only later that I fully realised how much stress and strain they had been under at various times.

My father was a very hardworking, honest and capable man, but was made redundant three times. He was proud of the fact that he never asked any other family members for help, and my mother recalls him going door to door for miles, looking for work. At one point he worked three poorly paid jobs simultaneously to sustain us, at others he suffered through posts with bullying superiors or through long commutes that gave him little time of his own. I learned to respect people who work because of his example, and that of my mother too, who worked a number of different menial jobs while raising us. I realise now that we were solidly working class, but my father never voted Labour in his whole life. We were the working class of the South, and I think my father knew as well as I did that Labour was not really on our side.

I get my politics from my father, but I suppose over the years my version of it has hardened. My father was a humanist, although he would not have used the term, and was interested in but not obsessed with politics. History occupied him more — that and nature, and the two combined in many discussions we had before he died. We both loved visiting castles, stately homes, old churches and any place steeped in English history, as well as woods, fields and farmlands. Although Essex is by no means associated with such things now, being linked more popularly with a brash, loud, unthinking kind of persona and with the clubs, bars and pubs in which that version of the county thrives, it is still in many places a very rural area, scattered with reminders of an ancient past. In the grounds of the castle in Colchester, you can visit the place where two Royalist commanders were executed during the Civil War, and in the castle itself, learn the Roman history of the town and where terrified Romans sheltered from the rampaging followers of Boudicca. In Rochford, there was once an estate belonging to Anne Boleyn's sister, whilst at Bradwell there is the oldest surviving Christian church in the country.

There are probably few places on earth with so much history which is so readily ignored as that found in the counties of England. You cannot escape it, from the old pavilion by the cricket field, through to the statues and war memorials of village greens, and even in the no longer smoky interiors of local pubs. But you can, unfortunately, ignore it. You can destroy it, too, if you have no care of such heritage, and we see that in churches converted into houses or nightclubs, or in memorials defaced and vandalised by ignorant youths. We see many of the institutions which once formed the traditional tapestry of life departing, from the working men's club to the village pub to the rarity, these days, of an English church with an actual congregation. Neglect and change destroy all things, eventually.

Going back to my original point, though, it is only recently that I found that caring about such things, and perhaps wanting to preserve some of what remains that made this nation unique, makes me an extremist. It always seemed to me that love of one's country, and respect for the people, places, events and forces that shaped it, was a very natural thing. It was like love of your family or respect for your parents. It was an extension of the pride you take in your own home, and the worry and care that you invest in your children. And this care you have for your own does not necessarily diminish the store of human kindness you have available for other places and other histories. My father, for instance, was fascinated with Native American history, and saw in some of the beliefs within those cultures similarities with the respect for Nature he had acquired personally. He loved the books of Grey Owl as well as those of Laurie Lee, both for their descriptions of the natural world and of man's place in it. But I suppose national feeling, whilst not diminishing compassion or respect, does prioritise it. We care more about our own family and friends. We care more too, many of us, about our own nation.

And then we found out what this care meant, to those who don't have it. We found out because of two events, several thousand miles apart, but similar in the seismic reactions they precipitated. These events were the election of Donald Trump and the Leave victory in the EU Referendum in the United Kingdom (also known as Brexit). In both cases, we saw a vote largely divided between what has been called the Somewheres and Nowheres. The Somewheres were people like me. They were more generally working class and they were, like me, concerned about the place they lived in. They were worried that it was changing, and not for the better. This concern took many forms. It was not just about immigration, although that was of course part of it. The Somewheres opposed mass immigration, the Nowheres supported it. But it was deeper than that. It was about whether you like the past and worry for the future, or whether you hate the past and don't worry about the future. Because all of that natural feeling for a nation that a Somewhere feels, a Nowhere does not.

A Nowhere, who might also be described as a Hillary voter or a Remain voter, largely does not share that sense of the specialness of a place as something to be cherished and protected. Nowheres do not have these feelings themselves and do not understand them in others. They invest, emotionally, in other concerns, identifying as Citizens of the World, as globalists, internationalists, and first and foremost as ideologues. Their political ideology, not their nation state, matters to them. Of course, many do love particular places, but they are likely to regard love of a nation as inherently irrational, if not actively evil.

There had, of course, always been this division to some extent, but it had been growing, the gulf between the two kinds of thinking widening. The nation state was one of the schism points, an obvious faultline between opposing world views. The Trump voter sees America as special, the Hillary voter does not. The Trump voter takes pride in the national story, the Hillary voter takes pride in rejecting the national story. And the same is true of Brexit. The Leave voter takes pride in Britain's past, the Remain voter sees that past as shameful. Neither side can comprehend how the other side reaches its conclusions. Both sides are emotionally invested in the truth of their vision.

Arguing over these events online, and over wider social issues relating to my traditional worldview, I encountered a huge amount of hate and active hostility, usually most vociferously from those who claimed to be speaking on behalf of progress and enlightened values. This was a surprising experience given my firm belief that my views were both natural and relatively moderate. I've never advocated political violence or racial discrimination, for example. But I came to realise that there are millions of people who consider the love of place, people and nation I had inherited as akin to the 'blood and soil' rhetoric of an actual Nazi. I found British people who admired Stalin and detested Churchill. I found Remain professors prepared to expound to pro-EU magazines on the inherent racial flaws of the English. I found websites dedicated to praising Communist dictators whilst demonising US presidents. And I did not have to go far to find countless slick media organisations spreading a daily diet of selective historical inaccuracies, or a mainstream commentariat losing all sense of reason and proportion in relation to the supposed evils of Trump and Brexit.

This experience seemed to bring into focus other things that had troubled me. I could not comprehend, for example, why there had been almost no mainstream comment when grooming gangs had raped thousands of children in the UK, in the heart of an advanced, supposedly caring liberal democratic country. How could that happen in a nation with such a highly developed welfare state, with scores and scores of charities, official bodies, police forces and social care organisations all claiming some remit to prevent such events? How could these things be ignored by everyone except those who, like me, were largely working class and worried about their area, and who were immediately labelled as 'far right' for what seemed to me to be the normal, healthy response of being horrified by the industrial-scale sexual abuse of minors? The lack of comment on this, combined with the following excess of comment on the slightest impolite wording by a Donald Trump or a Nigel Farage, spoke to me of two entirely different moral universes radically opposed to each other.

There was the moral universe I and most of the people I spoke to, who identified as right-wing, conservative or working class, inhabited. This was the universe that found grooming gangs far more worrying than Donald Trump, that found Stalin more evil than Churchill, that found love of your own country natural and hatred of it unnatural. This was the universe that was concerned about mass immigration and the changing nature of Western countries. It was the universe that thought that there are two genders, not dozens, determined by biology, not by choice. It was the universe that saw men and women as equal but different, and did not think that men were especially evil or that masculinity was 'toxic'. It was the universe that assumed that universities teaching the best writers of the past was what mattered, not that universities should teach only those writers that reflected the exact demographic composition of the present. It was the universe that went to work every morning, and didn't like or demand hand-outs and special advantages. It was the universe that knew that every colour and every race had good and bad within it, not the one that assumed that all evil stemmed from white people. It was the universe that saw actions as more significant than words, and would rather be offended than be controlled. It was the universe that accepted most of classical liberalism, and did not see any need to apologise for the history that had created those values. This universe did not riot, or protest. This universe voted, and expected the vote to be respected.

And then there is the other universe. In this opposing moral universe, the election of one flawed US candidate over another equally or more flawed one is the greatest disaster since the rise of Hitler. In this moral universe, it is just and good that a nation's intelligence services seem to be actively campaigning against its elected leader. It is a universe in which merely saying that someone is racist, or xenophobic, or mad, makes it so, without the necessity of providing any evidence other than another person making the same slur. In this moral universe, diversity is a kind of God that must be worshipped, unless of course it is diversity of thought, which must be crushed. Grooming gangs are nothing to be worried about, and neither is Islamic terrorism. The real evils are capitalism and banking, together with men who happen to be white. If they are old, white and heterosexual, their evil is assured, unless they have made their careers telling us that all other old, white, straight men are to be demonised.

In this moral universe, the only democracy in the Middle East is responsible for all the conflict in the Middle East. Terrorism would not exist without the rapacious evil of the US, whose insistence on buying and selling things destabilises the entire globe. In this moral universe, the West arbitrarily decides to bomb other nations, apparently in the belief that burning countries sell oil more cheaply. In this moral universe, men oppress women, straights oppress gays, whites oppress other races, and history is nothing but the catalogue of the evils of straight white men. In this moral universe, capitalism, a system of exchange with no force necessarily required, is far more evil than Communism, a system of redistribution which requires the forcible seizure of property.

This second moral universe is the one this book is primarily about. Because as I encountered strange ideas on a whole range of topics, topics with little logical connection at first glance (gender, race, class, nationality, history, biology), it became more and more obvious that the opposing moral universe, the generator of the alien ideas I might otherwise have dismissed as a mere surge in irrationality, had a kind of internal logic. It wasn't traditional logic, which most of its views fundamentally oppose. It was its own logic, as circular as that of any self-confirming delusion. It was a definite, particular political ideology at work.

If you have ever wondered why some people believe that black people cannot be racist, or that all white people are privileged, or why some people excuse the crimes of Islam but obsess on US foreign policy blunders, if you have wondered how someone can see a multi-millionaire athlete as oppressed but a raped working class child as not oppressed, it is not enough simply to dismiss these absurdities as part of the troubling self-blindness of the Left. These and many other examples, including ridiculous levels of hatred towards Trump and Brexit, can be understood as multiple occurrences of the same phenomenon, which is the political ideology of Cultural Marxism in action. To proponents of this ideology, you, I, and anyone who is not also a Cultural Marxist, is an extremist. Every traditional or conservative opinion, on any topic, is their target.

1

CLASSICAL CIVILISATION

"The science, the art, the jurisprudence, the chief
political and social theories of the modern world
have grown out of Greece and Rome..."

—Thomas H. Huxley, Agnosticism and
Christianity and Other Essays.

IT IS IMPOSSIBLE TO UNDERSTAND WESTERN
civilisation properly without an equal understanding of Classical civilisation. The literature, sculpture, architecture, poetry, history, politics, art and
economics of ancient Greece and Rome were the bones upon which the flesh
of our society was formed. For centuries this classical heritage remained an
integral part of our own experience and identity, preserved in education
systems that prioritised a Classical education over all other intellectual and
social influences. Western thinkers, writers and politicians, western orators,
statesmen and diplomats, had a deep and abiding awareness of this connection between our society and that of the Ancients. At many points of our
history, it would have been difficult for someone without a formal education
in the Classics to be taken seriously unless they both acknowledged this debt
and manifested it in the allusions and references they deployed, thereby

demonstrating that they had made some private effort to compensate for not acquiring this knowledge by formal means.

The Classics for a thousand years provided a golden storehouse of apt examples and pertinent illustrations of almost every political, philosophical, social or moral quandary a man might encounter. Certainly, by the 18th century, everyone, from the lowliest journalistic hack to the greatest Prime Ministers or Presidents of the 18th and 19th centuries, was skilled in both deploying these examples and understanding and critiquing their use by others. Such an intimate familiarity with the Classical wellsprings of Western civilisation marked out the gentleman from the boor, and the scholar from the fraud.

The influence of classical antiquity can be seen all around us even today, in the neo-classical buildings that deliberately replicated Greek and Roman architectural forms, whether these are public monuments, government buildings or stately homes. This influence can be seen in political institutions, such as the US Senate, and in Latin mottos for everything from college societies to football teams. It can be felt when we watch the Olympics, or any of the athletic sports that derive from our Greek forebears. It suffuses the history of Western art and theatre, and defined much of what existed as high culture in the West for centuries. Classical myths and legends are endlessly repeated in Western art, whilst modern poets still translate and refashion Homer, Virgil and Ovid.

But where the Classics once formed a tapestry of links between the modern West and its ancient origins, that is no longer the case. Many of the examples and figures which would have been familiar to almost every educated person of the 19th century count as obscure references today. In education, the priority of the Classics was first questioned and then openly mocked. Throughout the 20th century, study of this heritage, together with respect for its pervasive significance, declined. It does not form any standard part of the state-provided comprehensive education most children receive in the United Kingdom, for instance, and is usually treated as some kind of archaic or frivolous option. We are told that more practical subjects exist, pragmatic topics of greater utility and urgency than the study of the Greeks and Romans.

But what this achieves in effect is actually to divorce younger generations within the West from themselves. It severs their heritage, and diminishes their place in the world. It denies them the useful moral and political lessons of antiquity, and makes earlier centuries dependent on that heritage as alien to them as the very distant past. This has a real and immediate impact on young people's political choices in the present, because they neither know nor understand the heritage of the West. They do not strive to preserve today what remains of yesterday, neither do they learn from the errors of classical antiquity nor emulate its triumphs. They have moved from regarding their own past with respect, to regarding it with an unwarranted contempt, based on false and superficial readings supplied to them — readings which they, not having received an education in the Classics, are unequipped to challenge.

This shift was not an accidental one. It was the result of deliberate policy choices, and consequent upon specific ideological assumptions. Classics were not dropped from school curriculums without opposition or comment. They had been part of what was meant by 'education' for over a thousand years. Children in the age of Alfred the Great had received some of these lessons, all the way through to the age of Churchill. The decline of the social respect entailed by this sort of learning was deeply woven into the crisis of confidence in the West during the post-colonial period. This was especially so since colonial administrations had been amongst the most enthusiastic in seeing the lessons of the Classics as both noble and utilitarian pursuits — they simultaneously elevated the mind of the recipient and equipped them for colonial responsibilities.

In Britain, since knowledge of the Classical heritage of the West was an aspect of class, associated with a ruling aristocracy, denial of that heritage became considered a facet of egalitarianism, freeing all classes from ancient cultural shackles. The huge costs of jettisoning this heritage in terms of self-knowledge and self-respect were not recognised at all by the proponents of the change, and in some cases not even by the traditionalists themselves. Though the latter were alarmed at such seismic cultural shifts, foreseeing as they did that public discourse would be less refined, intellectual endeavour coarsened, and aesthetic treasures neglected, they failed to recognise that the ultimate consequence of these actions would be to deny Western Man ownership of who he was.

The effect was as damaging as it was largely unacknowledged. Rather than being a citizen with a history that could inform his choices, Western Man became a far more malleable amnesiac, ripe for believing whatever nonsensical version of his past was imparted to him by the very people who hated and dismissed his actual history. What had been practised, in the decline of the centrality of the Classics in education, was a kind of vast theft of identity, an ideological vandalism greater in scale than the physical vandalism that had accompanied the dissolution of the monasteries in the time of Henry VIII.

A practical illustration of the effect of this change, and indeed also an illustration of why those who supported it wanted it to happen, can be seen in the case of Enoch Powell's infamous 'river of blood' speech. It is not for nothing that the phrase 'like the Roman' occurs both in Powell's speech and in the title of the magisterial biography of him. Powell had been the youngest professor of Classics in British history. His education, both at school and at home, inclined wholeheartedly to the Classics and to a traditional reading of the lessons to be derived from the Classics. So steeped in this heritage was he that it may be said that Powell was the closest thing to a Roman that could be found in the 20th century. As such, he did what all great English orators had done for centuries, and peppered his thoughts and comments with classical allusions. Yet the awareness of this shared past had so declined by that time that these allusions made Powell's speech, when delivered, almost an alien artefact, and this is certainly truer today than it was then.

Then and now, Powell's speech repulsed those with no understanding of its nuances nor comprehension of its place in the tapestry of history stretching from Powell back to Cicero or Livy. His crime was not only to think like a Roman, but to think like an Englishman steeped in the heritage of the West, one who was sure that such a heritage was worth preserving. The deliberate philistines of the modern era, those who had chosen to abandon their history, could neither understand nor sympathise with such a mentality. Not even the most naturally patrician of them, Edward Heath, was able to do so.

In many senses, the delivering of Powell's speech can be seen as the last time a British politician attempted to defend Western Civilisation, using the traditional tools (Classical references and rhetoric) of Western heritage He was destroyed for doing so, just as those who denied the centrality of the Classics had intended. It is virtually impossible today for a mainstream political figure to do either. Perhaps the closest attempts in recent years to defend Western civilisation in the way Powell did may be seen to have been made by` Boris Johnson. However, the manner in which his Classics-influenced intelligence is united to a jolly, buffoonish public character tells you just how far Classics have fallen in common estimation (what was once seen as the height of educated gravitas now passes for avuncular slapstick). We have moved from seeing an awareness of this heritage as a mark of seriousness, a thing which showed that a man was equipped for the business of politics, to seeing it as the opposite, a mark of unworldliness and anachronism.

A cursory look at the divisions which emerged within the ruling class of the British political establishment to the threat of Brexit is illustrative of this point. Despite the pervasive Remainer assumption of social, intellectual and cultural superiority, very few prominent Remainers would be considered cultured in the understanding of genuine Classicists. Theirs is largely a superficial understanding of both British and European history, filtered through the bureaucratic lens of those few European cultural highlights (like 'Ode to Joy') European politicians favour. Nobody could seriously expect the likes of Clegg, Blair, Cameron or May to know much of anything regarding real European history, whereas Johnson both enjoyed and remembered the Classics he encountered. Leading Tory Brexiteer John Redwood for example, was both a trained and gifted historian. His contemporary party leader and re-emerged Europhile, John Major, was not. The self-professed Remain love of expertise goes missing when it comes to an actual familiarity with European history.

It is sadly the case that Classical references today fail to communicate to an audience stripped of all awareness of their meaning, and any robust defence of civilisation, wherever it appears, is quickly placed in a box labelled 'Far Right', a box rapidly filling with any opinion that is not Cultural Marxist in every way. We can see this in responses to speeches by the Hungarian Premier, Viktor Orban, or in reactions to Donald Trump's speech in Poland, both of which represent rare instances of Western politicians speaking about the most significant issue in Western politics, namely whether the West, in any meaningful sense, can continue to exist.

2

DEMOCRACY & TYRANNY

"The ship of democracy, which has weathered all storms,
may sink through the mutiny of those on board."

—Grover Cleveland

ONE OF THE KEY CHARACTERISTICS OF WESTERN
civilisation has been its reliance on a democratic model of governance, and
this is also of course one of the greatest and most obvious examples of the
inheritance of Ancient Greece. It was the Ancient Greeks who invented
and named democracy, the word being derived from 'demos' and 'kratos',
together meaning 'the rule of the people'. Greek democracy, particularly the
Athenian model, was very different to what democracy means today. Initially
perhaps no more than a show of hands in a public gathering of all citizens,
usually on a hill, amphitheatre or open space of a polis or city state, Greek
democracy was limited rather than universal. In most city states, women
were in a subordinate social position, whilst it was actually the Greek state
least associated with democracy, Sparta, that granted the greatest status to
women. The Greeks practised slavery of course, and slaves were excluded
from all political processes. But the idea of voting, and voting anonymously,
was invented by the Greeks. When a show of hands was replaced with the
counting of differently coloured stones deposited by citizens, the anonymity

of the voter was instituted, a requirement of what we consider free and fair elections even today.

Democracy has changed in significant ways within Western polities, especially via the gradual extension of the right to vote to initially excluded sections of society, whether those be persons who do not meet previous property requirements, persons younger than were traditionally consulted, or women. It also takes multiple forms via different political structures (the difference, say, between the US and the UK). But the key concepts remain: the idea that a leader is not born to rule purely by class but is chosen by an electorate, and the idea that one citizen has one vote, and that all citizens are consulted. These form the essence of democracy. That essence does not change. Today, however, perhaps more than at any time (apart from the interwar period that saw the birth of fascism), the value of democracy is increasingly questioned, the importance of democracy increasingly ignored, and the willingness to submit to alternatives greater than ever.

Opposition to democracy has always existed from two distinct sources which might otherwise be considered natural enemies. Both the natural elitist and the embittered revolutionary have a distaste for democracy. A section of the ruling class, that which persists in believing itself more fit to rule than the mass of mankind, and a section of the underclass, that which sees the political system as fundamentally unlikely to ameliorate its own condition, agree on the inequity inappropriateness of the rule of the common majority. The social class may differ, but the mindset is the same. The revolutionary thinks that he or she has a special insight, an ideology or belief system that justifies such things as violent action. The elitist alike considers himself or herself special, elevated above the masses, and able to make better decisions than those reached by elections or referendums, due owing to the possession of some special expertise or training consequent upon class and wealth. In both cases, the special quality is nearly always illusory, a projection of personal egoism rather than a politically meaningful distinction from others.

In reality, democracy united to capitalism has been the greatest engine of human progress in all history. The nations that have embraced both have flourished, while the nations that never embraced either have withered. The political and economic systems of democracy and capitalism have engaged and channelled the energies and genius of the greatest number of people, allowing the societies that followed these systems to flourish and out-compete those that did not. It is difficult to escape this conclusion if you look at the whole history of Western civilisation, but it is equally difficult to appreciate it if you do not.

In small, focused communities, direct democracy is easy to apply and its successes are more immediately obvious. The Ancient Greek city states, even the mightiest like Athens, Thebes and Sparta, were tiny in terms of population when compared with contemporary Western settlements, particularly in their earlier phases. Roman civilisation saw a spread of cities, but again few that could compare with a city today, whilst for centuries following the fall of the Western Roman Empire, it could be argued that Constantinople was the only great metropolis in the Western world, and even that was at its periphery. If, however, you live in a medium-sized population of 65 million persons, tied to a larger political entity of 500 million people, your solitary vote in that great mass becomes increasingly meaningless, both to you and to those who rule you. And if those who rule become or remain a distinct class, a nomenklatura united in their beliefs and practices, the benefits of democracy become less distinct. It is in this atmosphere that anti-democratic forces, both from within the ruling elite and from the disaffected underclass, can cohere in mutual opposition to the rule of majority opinion. This is of course exactly what we have seen with responses to the 17.4 million votes for Brexit.

As the Greeks gave us our understanding of democracy and its importance, they also gave us our understanding of what is meant by its opposite, tyranny. At first, this understanding was not purely pejorative. A Tyrant was merely a sole ruler, who could be and often was elected to precisely that position. In the Ancient World, societies vacillated between different systems of government much more readily than the larger, more complex societies of today are capable of doing. A Tyrant could be introduced as an emergency measure, to deal with some particular crisis in the polis, concentrating power until the emergency had passed. Totalitarian systems in more modern times universally allege the benefits of such concentration of power, and, indeed, it was a key part of every dictator's cult of personality. The Nazis asserted that Weimar democracy had failed because power was distributed amongst a range of self-serving politicians, all of whom were capable of being weak, incompetent or corrupt. Nazism was destined to defeat other European nations precisely because those nations were democratic, and therefore weak. Government could only deal effectively with a crisis when it was guided by one masterful intelligence.

Even in the ancient world, however, individual tyrants proved that they could create as well as solve disasters, and a firm suspicion of any lasting continuation of tyrannical rule was already a constituent of the Western mindset. Various Greek city states rebelled against internally or externally opposed tyrants, whilst the great resistance against Persia was, then and now, cast as a rejection of Eastern despotism, a version of extended tyranny. The Roman rejection of the Etruscan kings, and the subsequent care with which the title of 'king' was avoided by even the most autocratic emperors, is another pragmatic example of this key thread of Western political thought. Totalitarians in the West who oppose democracy, such as genuine Nazis or Communists, are in effect placing themselves in opposition to the entire history of the West, which has depended for its success on democratic forms and the societal energy these forms unlock.

Tyranny can best be understood as the absence of democracy. Any individual or system that moves away from democracy moves towards tyranny. But our understanding of what tyranny is has been warped by a more recent history of totalitarianism. In *1984*, George Orwell described a dystopian vision of a future Britain transformed into an overt tyranny. He described this as 'a boot stamping on a face, forever'. This is, of course, the version of tyranny we are most familiar with. It is the version that suffuses literature and film, and which essentially repeats the symbology and tropes of Nazism and, to a lesser extent, Communism. We see it in documentaries on the rise of Hitler. We see it in 'V for Vendetta'.

The paraphernalia is always the same. Marching, jack-booted militarism. Flags in procession and draping public buildings. Floodlights and book burnings, mass rallies and military parades. We identify tyranny through the presence or absence of these features, as if to be real, tyranny must follow the script of a film by Leni Riefenstahl (incidentally, referring to Greek-influenced athletic displays formed a key part of Nazi propaganda, and these athletic displays were of course central in Riefenstahl's 'Olympia'). Many of the features present in Orwell's work are actually more subtle than these overt forms of tyranny, particularly the ceaseless revision and subversion of objective history that forms Citizen Smith's employment. But the outer forms dominate public consciousness. The central place of WWII in 20th century history explains this, together with the strange and sickly fascination Nazi evils hold over the public imagination.

The disservice this fascination with overt tyranny does, however, is to blind us to the dangers of any manifestations of tyranny that are less overt. It removes the traditional Greek duality of tyranny and democracy, and makes it harder to recognise that moves away from democracy are movements towards tyranny. The other great dystopia of the mid-twentieth century, Aldous Huxley's *Brave New World*, deals with the other kind of tyranny, the subtle kind.

It is an important distinction. *Brave New World* imagines tyranny via a willing submission, as opposed to an unwanted oppression. Huxley's dystopia gives the majority of people exactly what they want — a superficial and in many cases artificial happiness. The key speech of the novel comes when an individual demands the right to be unhappy, recognising that the world of casual sexual liberation, easily satisfied material wants, and a chemical fog of unthinking pleasure is another kind of denial of essential freedom. This moment is mirrored in the discussion regarding the virtual environment in the film *The Matrix*, where a more cynical character accepts that an unreal steak is preferable to real gruel. Huxley was obviously thinking of American consumerism and instant gratification, but perhaps the right to engage unhappily in politics is also relevant. Democracy is not a utopia, but every utopian alternative has had a dystopian finale.

The effect of this recent history is to make those with no knowledge of the Greek and Classical origins of the very concepts of democracy and tyranny more susceptible to the substitution of one with the other, provided that that substitution is an act of legerdemain, more subtle in its execution than the stamp of a jackboot. Those ignorant of or disillusioned with democracy are fertile ground for the seeds of tyranny. With extremist totalitarian groups, the denial of democracy is obvious, overt and unashamed. This is true of Nazis, Communists and Islamists.

A greater danger, perhaps, is the widespread acceptance of some of these groups' anti-democratic aspects by those who don't belong to these radical groups. Nor is an increasing suspicion regarding the efficacy of democracy an accidental thing. We see it being deliberately fostered and spread by many of the elitist responses to Trump or Brexit, and we see it enshrined in the operating structure of the EU or the UN, where outer democratic forms (the existence of Parliaments, debating chambers and votes) mask a fundamentally anti-democratic agenda (at the national level). The EU is a perfect example of a form of subtle tyranny, whereby fundamental rights are suppressed in the name of fundamental rights or where a Parliament exists only to legitimise a higher authority that holds the real power, far away from the demos (reminiscent of the Roman senate under the worst Roman emperors).

3

CIVILISATION AND BARBARISM

"Youths of the Pellaians and of the Macedonians and of the Hellenic Amphictiony and of the Lakedaimonians and of the Corinthians...and of all the Hellenic peoples, join your fellow soldiers and entrust yourselves to me, so that we can move against the barbarians and liberate ourselves from the Persian bondage, for as Greeks we should not be slaves to barbarians."

—Alexander the Great

THE GREEKS GAVE US DEMOCRACY. THEY ALSO gave us civilisation, and the admittedly arrogant notion that there is a fundamental distinction between Western civilisation and barbarism. When the Greeks thought about what united and defined them, they were not primarily thinking of political institutions or shared methods of governance. They had the example of the huge gulf between the societal structures of Athens and Sparta to make it obvious to them that politics alone did not define what it meant to be Greek. The seed of the distinction between the Greek and the non-Greek was not political. It was not even racial, although that certainly played a part, and a more obvious and unashamed part than would be comfortable for many today. The key distinction was cultural, namely language.

The word 'barbarian' came from the sound of the non-Greek languages used outside of the Greek city states (a 'bar-bar' noise, according to the Greeks). To be a Greek, you had to sound like a Greek, deploying the same language in the same way. Even those who shared many other Greek characteristics were seen to be somewhat dubious if their speech and language marked them out as being significantly different. The Macedonians, for example, had pronounced accents that resulted in debates concerning whether or not they were genuinely Greek. A political dimension also figured in that doubt, given that the Macedonians favoured a more primitive (in Greek eyes) societal model of direct kingship (different from the dual kingship of the Spartans). Uniting other Greeks in conquest of barbarians was in part a Macedonian assertion of their own right to be considered Greeks.

If we compare this with imperial Western societies of the 18th and 19th century, the parallels in the significance of language and the mentality of defining civilisation in opposition to barbarism become most obvious. Received English pronunciation went hand in hand with the later stages of the British imperial mission, whilst the French retain to this day an extraordinary degree of sensitivity regarding the sanctity and significance of formal French. Language is one of the clearest markers of culture, which is why traditionalists value its proper expression and revolutionaries do not. But it is also one of the means by which culture is controlled and guided, by which society is shaped, and by which thoughts are both marshalled and controlled. An attempt to control language is always an attempt to control the boundaries of what is acceptable and unacceptable in thought. This is the process we see in operation when Cultural Marxists, in the manner of Citizen Smith, reshape the meaning of specific words, or institute an Orwellian double-speak regarding what a word claims to express and what it actually expresses (as in the phrase 'social justice').

Today it is almost impossible to conceive of a Western politician or leader, commentator or thinker who would give an unabashed and robust exposition of the idea that Western culture was in any way superior to any other culture. Contemporary liberal leaders in the West, by contrast, specialise in apologising for the supposed exceptional evils of Western society and history, as we see with the endless lachrymose apologies of Justin Trudeau on behalf of Canada or the Raj Apology Tour of the Blair years in the UK. Almost the only colonial history any of these contemporary liberal figures, or their audiences, will be familiar with are the touchstones of grievance, consisting of instances such as the Irish Potato Famine, which have been woven into the mythology of anti-colonialism and thereby anti-Western thought for more than a century. Those who have undergone a contemporary schooling receive no knowledge of the antiquity of Western culture and no understanding either of its essential characteristics or significant successes, both moral and practical. Instead, they will imbibe at best an anodyne relativism, at worst an essentially Marxist loathing of all traditional Western attainment.

The creed of multiculturalism is of course the practical application of the abandonment of Classical distinctions between civilisation and barbarism. Ancient Greek and Roman confidence in their cultural superiority inspired both artistic and military triumphs. The same self-assurance, learned from Classical examples, acted as a driving force of Western imperialism between the 15th to early 20th century. But a healthy society does not just impose its values on others, it refuses to allow its values and identity to be subverted by those opposed to it. It expects that the barbarian learn the rules of civilisation, and not that civilisation must submit to barbarian rule. This expectation can be couched with the greatest of politeness and still be a mark of cultural health and vigour, and is generally based on the idea that incomers to a society must integrate into that society by adopting loyalty towards it and its values.

Through most of Western history, this was an entirely uncontroversial operating principle of lawful migration, and the self-evidently damaging consequences of abandoning such an expectation would have been obvious to all. Only in the period in which classical liberalism gave way to contemporary liberalism, that is, only after WWII, was the disastrous idea that entire populations could be transferred, their primitive cultures intact, into civilised regions without any attempt at integration widely accepted (with predictably disastrous consequences). Greater awareness of the lessons of Classical antiquity would of course have made it obvious that multiculturalism was a policy without hope of a successful outcome, since the Romans had triumphed spectacularly when they made others Roman, and failed spectacularly when they did not. The late Western Roman Empire had even invited barbarian tribes in, who then contributed to Rome's fall.

The truth of the matter is, of course, that the Greeks and early Romans were correct, that the Classical Liberals of the 17th-19th centuries were equally correct, and that today's contemporary liberal and Cultural Marxist positions are incorrect. There is such a thing as a relevant distinction between civilisation and barbarism, there always has been, and there probably always will be, too. And even riven with self-doubt, even scarred by the psychic and social wounds of two devastating world wars, Western culture does remain superior to other cultures in a multiplicity of ways. Again, we did not lose sight of this truth accidentally. We were blinded to it, by world war guilt, but also by deliberate and malevolent Cultural Marxist teaching. Beginning perhaps with the crisis of faith, growth of anarchism, and end-of-the-century rejection of all traditional Western morality seen in the late 19th century, the most influential disseminator of the rejection of the hitherto accepted pre-eminence of Western cultural values was to be found in the revolution of attitudes in the educational establishment.

From the 1950s onwards, moral and cultural relativism, and a consequent disdain for the Ancient Greek categories of civilisation and barbarism, was not only promoted by academics but formed the new, thoroughly rigid orthodoxy of academic thought. Even on its own terms, it was selective and hypocritical, since whilst asserting that traditionalists must regard all cultures as equal it simultaneously concentrated entirely on the evils it detected within Western culture. These formed the basis of a significant proportion of all study in the humanities from that point on, and any scholar or student displaying the slightest jingoism, nationalism or cultural supremacism within their work would find it almost impossible to have that work, regardless of the critical acumen, depth of thought or thoroughness of research otherwise displayed, taken seriously.

At the same time, apparently unaware of the self-contradiction, the idea that one could and should negatively judge in moral terms the previous history of one's own culture took firm hold. Instead of rival cultures sharing the same timeframe, it was the Past that became the Other, Relativism reigned supreme in the Now, but all of the past was to be judged by purely contemporary standards. This directly inverted the established relationships which all Western cultures had held with antiquity (or indeed that the Greeks held with their own mythical Golden Age). Rather than being mindful in the present of the duty one owed to one's forebears, and of the awesome responsibility of protecting the cultural and political heritage they had passed on to us, academics and soon wider society following their lead decided that we were in fact the judges of the past in a never-ending trial of slanders and slights. If the Past could not conform to our present expectations, our ideologically-driven, Cultural-Marxist expectations, then we must as a moral and ethical duty condemn that past, despite the practical reality that such post-mortem condemnations serve no useful purpose other than to stimulate a righteous thrill in the hearts of the most fanatical of our contemporaries whilst alienating our society as a whole from many of its greatest achievements.

Traditionalists, of course, are instinctively aware of the hypocrisies of the contemporary position even if they do not explicitly articulate that awareness to themselves or others. They can sense that something is deeply flawed in this thinking. They retain an emotional and aesthetic bond with the great works of the past, and resent the crude intellectual philistinism which underpins the blanket dismissal of these achievements. Even if they have no particular artistic interest, they know that a Da Vinci sketch requires extraordinary skill and that a public urinal displayed in a museum as a pivotal work of art does not. They know that they are presented with a fraud, in ways that contemporary sophisticates, desperate to seem above the simple love of beauty and skill still prevalent amongst the masses, do not.

This instinctive awareness is ultimately the result of centuries of cultural learning, derived ultimately from the aesthetics of the Ancient Greeks, informed by generations to the point of being almost an inborn quality. It extends both backwards in time and geographically across borders, and a century of deliberate reversal and elite scorn has not revised or erased it. For the general public likewise knows that a crudely carved wooden statuette or fetish, an African tribal mask or a Native American totem, are simply not of equal attainment and worth as Shakespeare's King Lear, Michelangelo's David, or Mozart's Requiem. Relativism cannot abide the test of any meaningful aesthetic standard, since it is an inescapable fact that some cultures have achieved more than others. And this is true not only of art, but of science, of technology, of medicine, of philosophy, of military success, of economics and cultural values.

The prioritisation of non-Western cultures as equal or superior to ours is therefore an artificial construct (to use the Cultural Marxists' own phraseology) which is to objective critical enquiry as oil is to water. It is objectively true that a culture which still practices stoning is more barbaric than one that does not, and that a culture without ritual human sacrifice is more civilised than one with such practices. It is objectively true that Western culture has been responsible for more of mankind's greatest and most fundamental achievements in all areas than any other. We should never forget this. We should never cravenly apologise for our past or surrender our present.

We still know what makes the difference between civilisation and barbarism. We still know that civilisation is infinitely better for both the individual and for humanity as a whole. But civilisation is under enormous threat. It cannot and does not survive unless we are prepared to defend it, by word and deed. We start by rejecting the hypocritical relativism that Cultural Marxists seek to enforce. Instead, we engage in an active and continuing remembrance of what civilisation is, which is honouring and building upon the past, rather than traducing and desecrating it.

4

THE GREEK DEBT (PHILOSOPHY)

"It's my belief that history is a wheel. 'Inconstancy is my
very essence,' says the wheel. Rise up on my spokes if you
like but don't complain when you're cast back down into
the depths. Good times pass away, but then so do the
bad. Mutability is our tragedy, but it's also our hope. The
worst of times, like the best, are always passing away."

—Boethius, The Consolations of Philosophy

ALONG WITH THE CONCEPTS OF DEMOCRACY,
tyranny, civilisation and barbarism previously discussed, Western civilisation is most obviously indebted to the Ancient Greeks for the practice of
philosophy, and for the influence that philosophical movements have had
on the development of our societies. It is the Ancient Greeks who invented
the practice of philosophy and who prioritised the systematic search for
truth above the inherited traditions of religion. Philosophy was denied by
the early Christian church, its schools closed on the command of an emperor
guided by the vehemence of Christian mobs, but never quite destroyed,
and soon revived by clerical scholars and medieval scribes. For a thousand
years the most popular text in all the West, after the Bible itself, was *The
Consolations of Philosophy* by Boethius, a curious and moving amalgam of

Stoicism and Christianity that taught Europeans to endure and transcend worldly reversals.

The context of the birth of philosophy is significant. Pantheistic Hellenism was notable for a religious tradition in which the gods were quintessentially human in their vices, loves, lusts, sorrows and flaws, and in which many of the gods were to some extent caricatures of human emotion. Greek gods were perhaps written on a larger scale than mere mortals, but the language was the same. These were not unknowable or inscrutable beings, and whilst capable of appearing in any form, each form possessed a very human soul driven by fear or longing just like us. These gods did not love at a distance, but personally, vividly, lustfully. They were literal as well as figurative parents to humanity, or what humans with much greater power might well become.

At the same time, the Greeks elevated humanity itself into a form of divinity. First artistically, in aesthetic forms that obsessed on the perfection of the human figure, drawing closely from the elegance of forms of nature, whether those were the budding leaf, the curling vine, the slope of a shoulder, the fall of a woman's hair or the taut buttocks of youth. Secondarily, and equally naturally, they began to question their too human, too fallible gods, and elevate human consciousness itself in place of all such divinities. Without ever fully casting aside these older explanations and mythic conceptions of the universe and its operations, they began the process of applying pure human intellect to a whole range of social and political issues, as well as to their general understanding of abstract concepts.

We know where this process was initiated, and when. It was in Miletus, one of the Ionian Greek city states on the coast of what is now Turkey, in the fifth and sixth centuries BC, home of Thales, Anaximander and Anaximenes, who along with others form the group of very earliest philosophers who merit the term, in contrast to the sages, scholars and wise men who preceded even them and retained a theological conception of the world and of man's place within it. These earliest philosophers are referred to as the Presocratics, and only the slightest fragments of their work, often cryptic allusions and broad maxims recorded by much later commentators, survive. But what even these fragments make clear is that these men were as Aristotle later put it, *physici*, men who sought physical rather than spiritual explanations of all things. We know, too, that this represented a seismic shift in human understanding, unparalleled even by the brightest thinkers of other ancient civilisations.

Babylonians had charted stars with mathematical precision, and Egyptians had experimented in a crude sense and developed medicines and engineering sufficient to prolong the lives of great Pharaohs or build the mighty tombs in which they were lain, but in every instance the sturdy but crude beginnings of civilisation were wrapped in a shroud of theological thinking. The Egyptians knew effective herbs and remedies, but accompanied these with spells and incantations, for instance, or tiny scrolls on which praises were made to various divine beings. The Babylonians' great literary work is the tale of one king's search for immortality and descent into the underworld. The Presocratics could speak in riddles, but they did not speak a language dominated by gods and goddesses. Even if the only debt we owed them was to these earliest of philosophers, the scale of achievement is difficult to fathom, but when united with the entire subsequent history of philosophy, with the works of Aristotle and Plato, let alone the medieval Neo-Platonists or their contemporary descendants, we can see that philosophy to some extent formed a bank of the river of western history, guiding its path in unique and intellectually nourishing directions. It does not take a Boethius to be aware of the consolations of philosophy or of the debt owed by subsequent generations to these remarkable Ancient Greeks or the culture from which they came.

So what is it, exactly, that Ancient Greek philosophy has given us, and why is it something to be cherished and reminded of particularly in a period in which so much of Western cultural identity is under assault from Cultural Marxists determined to deny its importance and denigrate its achievements?

More than anything, the Greek philosophers gave us a unique mode of thought and discourse that equipped us to advance, technologically, scientifically and politically, more rapidly than other cultures. They gave us first the instinct to separate religion and thought, the desire to seek for non-religious explanations and to challenge any authority that rested solely on tradition. This thread passed into the later concept of the separation of Church and State, which eventually helped to free western society as much as was possible from the worst excesses of religious conflict (with notable exceptions).

This fundamental ability to separate the secular from the divine was not the only gift provided by Greek philosophers. They gave us in more general terms the spirit of enquiry, and respect for intellectual innovation, assuring original thinkers of a social context in which their most productive ideas could take root and flourish. They gave us a methodology sure to lean towards utilitarian results, practical and usable discoveries and inventions based on close observation of the physical world (not least in military applications, from the siege defences of Archimedes to the Greek fire, many centuries later, of the Byzantines). They gave us the tools of rhetoric, logic and the Socratic method, the balance of thesis and antithesis to form synthesis and the beginnings of the scientific method. They showed us that false ideas could be exposed by the simplest of questions striking at root causes and issues, and that great ideas could be formulated via a series of tests and confirmations. They showed us the difference between logical and methodical analysis and thoughtless presupposition.

Even today, the Socratic method is often the best means of exposing bad ideas. Even today, Cultural Marxists detest and devalue this heritage because it provides effective ammunition against their trite and hypocritical reasoning. Those who seek to debate or deny contemporary shibboleths can learn to do so by re-familiarising themselves with the philosophical heritage of the West. Learn how to deploy logic and rhetoric from a direct study of as many ancient Greek sources as you can acquire. They moved society away from barbaric modes of theologically driven thinking in their own age. They can do so again, in ours.

5

THE ROMAN DEBT (LAW)

"Much has been disputed about the 'ghost of the Roman Empire'
that still lurks far beyond the shores of the Mediterranean. The
heritage of Roman law is not a ghost but a living reality. It is
present in the court as well as the market-place. It lives on not only
in the institutions but even in the language of all civilised nations."

—Justinian I, The Digest of Roman Law:
Theft, Rapine, Damage & Insult

IF THE GREEKS PROVIDED WESTERN CULTURE
with its key mythological, philosophical and artistic roots they did the same
for the people of antiquity who most obviously supplanted them, the Romans.
Roman gods were at their core Greek gods, although the ever-pragmatic
Romans were always willing to endlessly add any local deities they encoun-
tered in Romanised forms. The intellectual currents of Roman life followed
Greek paths, as ever adding to rather than opposing existing forms. The
Greeks were the great creative intelligence of the ancient world; the Romans
were the great adapters and refiners of things already discovered by others.
We see this not only in mythology and art but also in philosophy, with
Romans as late as Marcus Aurelius and beyond adding to the established
Greek schools rather than forging entirely new paths. This is not to denigrate

Roman achievements, indeed it can be said to be a kind of national genius to successfully incorporate other influences whilst remaining true to yourselves and distinctly recognisable as a coherent identity of your own.

The Romans only made a significant break from Greek culture with Constantine's adoption of Christianity as the state religion, and in the Eastern empire of the Byzantines that followed, Greek identity once again surpassed Roman in a synthesis that united Greek language and ethnicity with devout Christian worship. The closure of the Greek symposia and academies, particularly in the great cultural centre of Alexandria, by early Christian emperors and mobs, represents one of the most barbaric acts of devout cultural vandalism one can charge Christianity with, but even then Christian liturgies, rituals and monks were vital in retaining what knowledge of antiquity survived. Byzantine scholars fleeing Muslim conquest would eventually reignite the Western awareness of Greek and Roman works, helping, amongst other things, to spark the creative ferment of the Italian Renaissance. Much Western history can therefore be understood as a cyclical process of loss and rediscovery of Greek and Roman sources of inspiration.

The debt that Western civilisation owes to the Romans is more complex and subtle, perhaps, than that it owes to the Greeks. The Romans gave Western culture a sense of imperial purpose which the Greek example of the heroics of Alexander, alone, might not have supplied. Greeks were significant traders before they were conquerors, and Romans were conquerors before they were significant traders. The Greeks provided a template to later westerners of how to think and feel, whilst the Romans provided a template of how to organise and rule.

This is the distinction that the Enlightenment-era tax rebels who formed the United States acknowledged in their mirroring of Roman political forms rather than Greek ones. The US system would have no basileus, for example, and certainly no tyrant, but it would have a Senate. Like the Romans, the Americans would begin by ousting a monarchy, with George III reprising the role of the Etruscan kings rejected by Republican Rome. Like the Romans, they would forevermore deny the authority of all kings and unite a key strand of their stubborn self-identity with republicanism and suspicion towards monarchical or absolutist rule. Perhaps more than anything the Americans would take on the Roman imperial mantle of manifest destiny and self-belief, formalising it through such measures as the Monroe Doctrine (claiming a sort of imperial protector role over Southern America akin to Roman treatment of neighbouring smaller states) and enacting it through eventual interventionism in both world wars.

British imperialism, by contrast, could be divided into two distinct phases. The early organic growth of Empire via trading colonies and the protection of trade routes was much closer to the model of the Athenian hegemony (like the brief Athenian ascendancy being based on trade and naval power and a semi-forced alignment of interests with existing regional powers). Early British imperialism was Greek in nature, whereas later British imperialism (the scramble for Africa and the direct seizure of additional territory by treaty or war) more Roman. Britain had to grow into that Roman sense of destiny over centuries of success, whereas the Americans felt it from the very beginning and signalled it in their political nomenclature.

Roman imperial destiny also had a separate meaning on the continent of Europe from that which it held for the British or the Americans. There has throughout Western European history been a sense that the collapse of the Roman Empire was a great mistake, a point at which history took a fundamentally wrong turn. Every pan-European project since has tried to reverse that error, to recreate the united political landscape of the Western Roman Empire. The Holy Roman Empire made such a comparison about as obvious and explicit as it could possibly be, but it was an ambition shared by most of those who have ever tried to enforce political authority throughout Western Europe. It is the ambition, essentially, that was held by Charlemagne, by Philip II of Spain, by Louis XIV, by Napoleon, by Kaiser Wilhelm II, by

Mussolini and, of course, by Hitler. It is the ambition and the sense of loss that informs the EU. Whilst the ambition can be united to radically different political projects, the model of what can be achieved remains the geographic borders of the former Roman Empire, and the inherent belief that it can or should be achieved derives from the knowledge of that lost European cultural and political unity.

Proponents of European integration under the EU today seem unaware of the imperialist nature of the project they support, but nevertheless view Brexiteers and Leave voters in the same way that a convinced supporter of Rome viewed the rebellious tribes of the Iceni. For a Remain supporter, Western civilisation is not defined by the shared cultural heritage derived from Greeks, Romans and Christianity, it is defined by the shared political hegemony of the EU which mirrors the geographic extent of the Roman Empire. The contemporary and artificial bureaucratic construct has become, for them, civilisation, and the older constituent nation states within the EU, and loyalty towards them, barbarism. Again, this can be viewed as a difference between Greek and Roman conceptions, between willing alliance against an external tyranny (Greek opposition to Persia) and enforced unity under economic or political authority (Roman power).

It should be remembered, however, that if their power was ultimately imposed militarily the Romans were also convincing persuaders. No empire can survive as long or spread as far as the Roman Empire did without offering a carrot as well as a stick to those it seeks to rule. The Romans were the best integrationists in imperial history. This is what I mean by saying that they gave a model of how to rule. The Roman response to external threats or newly conquered territories was consistent through much of their history, only breaking down in the final century of their collapse. To those that persisted in opposition, they offered complete annihilation, most notably in the instance of their Carthaginian competitors.

Oppose Rome and destruction follows. This is what they did to Thebes, for instance, to break Greek resistance. But accept Roman rule, accept Roman culture, and just as surely as destruction follows from resistance, rewards flow from obedience. Practical benefits would inevitably follow from becoming part of the Roman world. Underfloor heating, fine villas, exotic foods and flowing wine, access to increased education, higher status, more trade, aqueducts, roads, newly founded cities, all stamped the land and marked the minds of freshly conquered territories. Such benefits were particularly noticeable to those already from a complacently accepting ruling class. These individuals, if supportive of Rome, had their rights and privileges confirmed and immediately began to access practical benefits from Roman rule. In turn they then persuaded the rest of their populations that such rule was beneficial.

Rebellions against Roman rule derived largely from those very rare instances where some rash, corrupt or sadistic Roman ruler deviated from this policy (as in the case of Boudicca's revolt or much later troubles with unintegrated barbarian tribes settled in Roman provinces). In both their long successes and their ultimate decline, the Romans presented a treatise on both the ways to rule which will work and the ways that will fail. Not knowing these events, not learning from these examples, of course makes failure more likely, which is precisely why Cultural Marxists always attempt to separate western populations from widespread familiarity with their own history in antiquity.

The final way in which the Romans gave subsequent powers a lesson in rule is via the two greatest gifts that Rome could offer conquered territories. There is only one thing more persuasive than trade or power, and that is peace. Rome offered the Pax Romanum, an assurance of peaceful existence for those who submit. It is the same offer that the British gave to their territories when they were the leading imperial power. It is extraordinarily persuasive because so many other benefits flow from it. All the destruction of war is avoided, the disturbances of burnt crops, fallow fields, slaughtered sons and raped daughters are avoided. And the means by which this peace and security is offered is called law — the rule of law. For no matter how tyrannical an individual Roman emperor might be, he was still to some extent constrained by law, and it is Roman law which forms the basis of contemporary law throughout much of the Western world. Roman law is the foundation stone of Western law.

The idea that all men are limited in their actions by law, which is the codified means of preserving peace and goodwill between all men and harmonious relations within society as a whole, is an idea that has occurred, too, in non-Western societies (particularly in Chinese Confucianism). But Rome made that idea more real, Rome wrote that idea down, Rome lived by that idea and died by its transgression. Even in departing from that idea, Rome gave the West a lasting example of the dangers of absolute rule. A Nero, a Caligula or a Commodus told us what happens when those who rule are not restrained by any law greater than themselves, whilst an Augustus, a Hadrian or a Marcus Aurelius tell us how successful those who rule with respect for both natural and created law can be.

6

REASON

*"The state of nature has a law of nature to govern it,
which obliges every one: and Reason, which is that law,
teaches all mankind, who will but consult it."*

—John Locke, Second Treatise on Government

PART OF THE EDUCATIONAL GROUNDING THAT
Western civilisation used to impart to all educated persons was centred on
the notion of Reason. Reason is the power of thinking in an orderly and rational manner, usually by a series of connected steps which are verifiable and
subject to confirmation. We display the capacity to reason when we prioritise
a logical deduction over an immediate emotional reaction. Scientific enquiry
depends upon the ability to reason, as does critical analysis of society, literature or politics. It was once widely supposed that the capacity to reason is
what distinguished mankind from the rest of the animal kingdom, although
research on the possible thinking processes and decision-making activities
of some animal species has blurred these distinctions.

The use of tools, for example, manifests an ability to look at a problem
and create a solution based not on instinctive reaction but on some kind
of process of internal rationalisation and examination of options. Tool use
might in some circumstances derive from an intuitive leap of imagination,

but in others from exactly the kind of orderly process of thought we mean by reason. Crows, apes, monkeys, otters and eagles, among other species, have all been tested in the process of tool use, to varying degrees (an ape's use of a long blade of grass to dig out ants being a more obvious case of tool use than a bird dropping a hard-shelled prey against a rock from a great height). Early hominids distinguished themselves as masterful tool users and inventors, providing an additional evolutionary weapon that may well have been key to the difference between extinction and survival.

Throughout Western history, Reason as a Platonic abstract concept had periods of ascendancy and decline with regard to its cultural influence. It is not something strongly associated with theocratic societies, since solutions and practices in such societies are derived from priestly or divine command and instruction. This leads to potential social stagnation or even direct opposition to results derived from the application of reason, as occurred, for example, during the supremacy of the Catholic Church, with inventions or discoveries that seemed to question biblical or Papal sources. The Greeks in some senses invented the cultural understanding we have of Reason, and certainly deployed it far more than many other cultures, despite being also a people with a passionate and sensuous character. Respect for reason tends to peak during periods of cultural and artistic confidence, especially when societies test and break the limits of traditional theological restraint. We see this process repeatedly in Western history, far more so than in other societies.

The Renaissance, the Reformation, and the Enlightenment are the prime examples of this process, but smaller shifts in cultural direction, or less florid bursts of creative growth, show the same characteristic rise in regard for the human capacity to reason and in Reason itself as a concept. Perhaps the height of such regard came in the 18th century, where Reason was elevated to a higher level of respect than ever before. At this point in history, Western man became confident that Reason would eventually solve any problem or remove any societal ill. Reason dominated even such emotive areas as courtship and poetry, with the carefully constructed, the clever, the painstakingly crafted being regarded with greater respect than the intuitive or purely emotional. But almost as soon as this ascendancy had been achieved, and at the very point that Reason itself was deified in the midst of the French Revolution, Western civilisation was given a salutary reminder of the old Stoic principle that all forms of excess are more negative than restraint. Enlightenment Reason, taken to its ultimate extreme, gave us Revolutionary Terror.

Literary movements often give us a foreshadowing of political developments, even when the texts in question are not always explicitly political. Thus we see the crisis of Reason in the political sphere presaged by a shift from the witticisms and mannered satires of the Ancien Régime and neighbouring polities (such as the meticulous poems of a Pope or the philosophical reflections of a Voltaire), reacted against by the rise of Gothicism and Romanticism. Enlightenment Reason birthed its own antithesis. Societies still gripped by hierarchical and traditional structures of power produced the literature of the transgression of all morality, Gothicism, with its florid and voyeuristic portrayals of the breaking of societal taboos (such as the infamous scene, found in *The Monk* by Matthew Lewis, depicting the hero's incestuous coupling with his sister on a bed of corpses).

In the figure of the Marquis de Sade we see the logical end point of a rebellion against traditional taboos, with a writer who chose to live as well as write a manifesto of perversities. Sadism, and the supremely selfish satisfaction that comes from seizing whatever pleasures we like no matter the cost to others, is the dark counterpoint of the Enlightenment — the valuing of Man above God, the individual above the collective, the new and intense above the old and dull. The Marquis, of course, was also a hero to many of the political revolutionaries who sought the same toppling of established rule in the political sphere that he had championed in the sphere of human sexuality. This was a perfectly understandable development, given that the political and the sexual extremist are both the enemies of Reason and of traditional Western morality. We will never know exactly how many political extremists derive a sadistic sexual pleasure from the cruelties their creeds require, but it is probably a significant psychological stimulus and part of the appeal of such movements to a certain type of person.

In modern times, of course, we also see this unification of sexual freedom and political extremism. What was once a necessary movement towards equal treatment within society for those with harmless sexual orientations that were traditionally frowned upon has become an entirely selfish quest for enhanced rights and status by an explicitly political movement of sexual supremacists. Modern feminists no longer address existing injustices against women, since most of these have been addressed or are illusory in Western society, but prefer to create new injustices against men. Specifically, white men. Thus we see that the extreme race-guilt theory of 'White Privilege' was created by a feminist academic. Similarly, we see the LGBT movement justifying its continued existence after sexual liberation via an ever-expanding list of purely mythical oppressions, such as the notion that someone not using recently invented and arbitrarily decided upon pronouns is a form of aggression, or that not accepting the entirely evidence-free assertion that we are a species of more than two genders is also some form of psychic assault.

In these examples, we can see that modern sexual politics is predicated on a fundamental rejection of traditional Reason, just as some literary and artistic movements have been, and just as Sadism or Satanism are. Reason requires us to adhere to objective realities, to the tested, the proven, the measurable. Sexual identity politics is now based entirely on subjective emotionalism and tribalistic hysteria, rejecting even the basic scientifically verified facts regarding human biology. Reason has never been under such sustained assault, for even the Romantics or the most lurid Gothicist did not think to deny the physical reality of basic human categories. They might have denied limits on sexual behaviour or scorned traditional gender roles, but they did not invent new genders at will.

7

LOGIC

*"Consequently he who wishes to attain to human
perfection, must therefore first study Logic, next the
various branches of Mathematics in their proper
order, then Physics, and lastly Metaphysics."*

—Maimonides

IF REASON CAN BE DESCRIBED AS THE STRATEGY
of objective thinking, or perhaps the truest expression thereof, then Logic is
the tactical means by which such a strategy is achieved. Logic and Rhetoric
once formed the two strongest pillars of a Western education; they were
the reliable supports on which the entire edifice depended. Logic is a path-
way the reasonable mind prefers to follow, by inference from known and
confirmed facts to general judgements that naturally follow. The secondary
truth follows naturally from the first and is therefore neither an assumption nor an emotional reaction, but a kind of most plausible possibility.
It can be subject to further tests for verification, and could still be wrong
if formative data is missing or inaccurate, but has a greater likelihood of
discovering unknown truths or general principles than any purely intuitive methodology.

We use logic when extrapolating from statistical data to conclusions drawn from such statistics, and it therefore serves an obvious and significant role in the sciences. But it is also a key component of traditional academic method, a tool of informed discussion, a habitual feature of any intellectual endeavour that involves systems or processes of understanding. Rhetoric requires the use of logic combined harmoniously with the appeal to emotion in the language of politics or social persuasion.

We can even say that it is in the interplay of logic and emotion that the pattern of great oratory is found, as in the speeches of a Cicero, a Churchill or a Martin Luther King. Great speeches have an air of inevitability about them, which derives from the logical construction of an emotional point. When we respond to such speeches, we do so as if we have voiced the next line, internally, before it is spoken. Everything in a great speech is original, but none of it is surprising. We know the logic of it, in our hearts as well as our minds. The great political speech is in one sense the most human of all creative endeavours, because unlike any other, it wholly depends on this marriage of opposites which reflects the fundamental truth of our own human nature, always divided against itself between heart and mind, brain and spirit, reason and emotion. The speech seems true, even if it isn't, because of this underlying truth, this momentary sense that our divided nature is healed, our contradictory selves united in a moment of clarity.

This is why we also talk of a speech having or embodying a vision, and of the greatest political speakers being visionaries, since in the moment of that speech we are gifted with a clarity of perception we do not normally possess. We see the speaker's mind, and through that, a coherent view of the world, often more coherent than our own. Great literature does this too, of course, but usually more subtly, perhaps more deeply, over a longer period. The great political speech is an explosion of vision, whilst the great novel is a lingering voyeur.

In a period in which Reason is devalued, so too is Logic. A neglected house has an overgrown path to the front door. But like much else we are discussing, this neglect is not accidental, nor is it, as it was under Romanticism, a primarily aesthetic affectation. Cultural Marxism cannot sustain itself by logic, since there is nothing logical in the notion that one should emotionally and absolutely reject every element of one's cultural heritage and established history. Rather, this political ideology needs logic to be discredited, devalued and ignored. This process was fundamental to the current successes of Cultural Marxism within our society, particularly its dominance of academia.

Academics, by the old classical liberal version of what it means to be an academic, should be the most logical thinkers in our society, those trained to carefully weigh and evaluate all ideologies and opinions by reference to both objective reality and fundamental moral truths. Nobody should be more reasonable, and more trained to think in accordance with the dictates of logic, than an academic. We know, however, that the situation today is the exact opposite of this ideal scenario. Academics have been at the vanguard of the assault on Western civilisation, and have become in the main vigorous opponents of logic. Logocentrism, according to the contemporary academic, is only another means by which Western civilisation devalues and debases others (who are always assumed, in the fashion of Rousseau, to have a primitive authenticity Western man lacks).

Logic is, like everything else in the mind of the Cultural Marxist, about power. Their own obsession with claiming power, with the authoritarian instinct to control what others think and do, leads them to suppose that all history is about the interplay of power structures, and all proven beneficial cultural memes are merely devices by which some rule and some don't. Even the obviously practical necessity of identifying those whose mental processes make them a clear danger to others, that is, the treatment of the insane, becomes, according to Foucault, nothing but an exercise of power. The fact that most societies have a general internal accord regarding what constitutes insanity, shared by the powerful and the powerless alike, is seen not as proof that there might objectively be such a thing as insanity, but merely as verification of the manner in which all of society is unjustly dominated by the power, intellectual as well as physical, of the ruling elite. Insanity is simply a label applied to those who are dangerous to the social conventions and existing power structures of a given time.

Like all the most convincing lies, there is some truth to this worldview, in that regimes can and indeed have pathologised political dissidence, although the Soviets engaged in this practice far more than the European monarchies Foucault more frequently discussed. And, of course, Cultural Marxists themselves engage in this form of exclusion and demonisation very readily, as they have via repeated slurs regarding the mental stability of Trump or, more generally, in the creation of words like 'Islamophobia'. As is if often the case, Cultural Marxism accuses Western civilisation of a negative practice (the pathologising of political dissent) which Cultural Marxism itself deploys far more frequently. This transference of sin is a common feature of Cultural Marxist reasoning.

The Cultural Marxist rejection of logic therefore serves a twofold purpose. First, there are few logical arguments in support of any form of Marxism. Every society that has tried Marxism has experienced tyranny, since property cannot be redistributed without first being seized, and any such seizure requires the use of force. By rejecting logic, Cultural Marxists do not lose a weapon that forms any part of their own arsenal in debate. They are far happier with arguments that are based on utopianism at best, demonisation at worst. Their thinking is Manichean, dominated by secular versions of the heavenly and the demonic, determined by pure emotion and then memorised by rote. They are theocrats without a named God. Any mind trained in logic will itself reject such thinking, without requiring any external oratory to do so.

It logically follows, for example, that every human society in history that refuses to defend itself from external threats or that has no sense of loyalty or self-preservation falls to more confident opponents. Basic awareness of the nature of competition alone, let alone historical knowledge of the fate of fallen societies and now-defunct civilisations which have been conquered in one way or another by others, would cause a reasonable, logical mind to retreat from the self-defeating aphorisms of Cultural Marxism. This leads to our second point regarding the hostility of Cultural Marxism towards logic. A society in which logic is not esteemed is a society ill equipped to resist the illogical arguments on which Cultural Marxism depends. The Cultural Marxist does not want logic for himself, because it is a tool he neither understands nor can readily deploy. But, more importantly, he does not want it available to others, because he still has some dim perception that those equipped with logic are inoculated against his reasoning and armed against his verbal assaults. Worse yet, a trained logician or a society in which logical reasoning is prevalent cannot ever succumb to the authority of his creed. For this reason alone, if no other, logic must die.

8

THE SCIENTIFIC METHOD

"Hurrah for positive science! Long live exact demonstration."

—Walt Whitman, *Leaves of Grass*

THE SCIENTIFIC METHOD IS A MORE FORMAL CODI-
fication of the process of enquiry begun by the Ancient Greek philosophers.
It is also the single greatest cause of the technological and scientific fecundity
of the West, especially in comparison to other regions and the different
cultures within them. It is an indisputable historic fact that the West has
contributed more of the practical building blocks of modern existence than
any other culture. Most of the science and technology which we today take
for granted only exists as a consequence of the scientific method invented in
the West, and the majority of human technology and science was discovered
or invented by Western thinkers. Of course, other cultures can also have a
proud record when it comes to technological development, particularly the
Chinese but also the Japanese and to a lesser extent those working within the
Golden Age of Islam, but none of these other sources of scientific advance
have the same remarkable body of discoveries and achievements to cite as
Western civilisation. The argument that they do or that they are in any sense
more significant than the West when it comes to technology and science is
simply false.

The Chinese made significant discoveries considerably earlier, such as the printing press, the chemical and physical reactions necessary for explosives and fireworks, or the process for creating porcelain, but the static, deeply tradition-focused nature of the Chinese imperial system under successive dynasties led to the failure of these individual instances of technological achievement to cohere into a dynamic science-oriented inventiveness equal to that of the West. Thus, whilst China could produce populous cities with high levels of social stratification, cultural development and infrastructure, together with the capacity to engage in enormous engineering projects requiring advanced technical expertise, such as the Great Wall, we see these developments having far less impact on the nature of the society as a whole, and on subsequent technology, than innovations introduced into Western societies. This was indeed the case with other ancient societies which had led the way in the initial process of moving from traditional nomadic or agrarian societies towards stratified urban-centred cultures (which were nevertheless still primarily rural in population and traditional in outlook; city dwellers outnumbering rural dwellers overall is an entirely modern phenomenon).

It is an interesting question as to whether the difference between the ability of ancient cultures like Egypt, China and the Indus Valley civilisation to create large urban centres and specialised technically proficient trades without experiencing the kind of seismic cultural shifts we see in the West when major technological breakthroughs occurred is a positive or a negative trait. In terms of the short-term stability of these cultures, we must acknowledge that slow or static technological process probably increases cultural longevity overall, and that if the primary aim of a culture is, like some unthinking bacillus, to preserve and repeat itself, then in the medium term such stasis, usually enforced by absolutist hierarchies, is a very successful strategy.

The trouble with such a strategy is that when faced with more dynamic cultures that do survive, with competitors that can integrate your technology and swiftly improve upon it or make their own discoveries at a much more rapid pace, internal stability provides little defence against the external threat. This is one of the reasons why China eventually became the humiliated plaything of more technologically developed Western rivals that it still regarded as primitive barbarians. Even before that, the swift military innovations of Mongol horse warriors could outperform a far more developed China, leading to conquest and submission. Again, there are obvious geopolitical lessons here for Western civilisation today. Stasis represents eventual death, but so does too rapid change. The development of society must occur at an organic rather than artificial pace, and it is a foolish ruling class which either bars all change or welcomes any change regardless of consequence. Ancient China or the Shogun-era Japan that barred foreign traders are examples of one extreme at the overly conservative end of this spectrum, whereas contemporary Western liberalism represents the other extreme.

One of the factors that makes the difference in managing the inevitable change of society is of course the scientific method, which places man in a new relationship with both the natural and invented world. That is, the scientific method trains the Western mind, or the mind of any other culture that adopts it, to process the experienced world in a utilitarian fashion. If a plant has medicinal properties, for example, a traditional shaman might well be aware of that, and a culture without the scientific method will still develop cures and therapies based upon that knowledge. But these will be wrapped in superstition and cant, or ascribed to mystical, spiritual or divine origins (such as the plant being sacred to a particular deity, or formulaic incantations being as necessary a part of the cure as the plant itself).

The scientific method, by contrast, will not interact with such traditional knowledge in a static fashion, merely passing down what has been inherited from others. It will add personal interaction and experimentation. The plant will be studied minutely, to discover from exactly where the healing properties derive. If different parts of the plant have different properties, these will be examined and listed. Experimentation will confirm the effects of different doses and concentrations in different circumstances. All of this is more active and expands understanding far more rapidly than mere repeated usage, although that in itself becomes a kind of slow experiment. What the scientific method does, primarily, is to shift the development of knowledge from the accidental to the deliberate. Whilst many great discoveries (such as penicillin) are fortuitous, the possibility of such good fortune is inherently increased by the process and expectations of the scientific method and the running of multiple experiments. It is deliberately repeating in the space of ten days of close observation what might otherwise require one hundred years of accident.

In an odd way there is a direct contradiction between what the scientific method does, and what it allows. In using the scientific method, we observe and infer, we test our inference and observe again, and we repeat the entire process to confirm. We must spend time observing nature as closely as possible. We form an idea as to what might be happening or why, then we test that idea in multiple ways. We form conclusions that come logically from this process of observation, experimentation, and testing, and we devise means by which these conclusions can be confirmed or denied. All of this, individually, takes time and patience.

The chief personal characteristics of the greatest scientific minds are often curiosity and patience — the desire to know combined with the patience to keep asking the necessary questions. Someone such as Darwin, for example, could display a supernatural degree of individual patience, readily sacrificing years and decades of life testing a single idea. How many of us really possess either the burning curiosity or the excessive patience required to study earthworms every day for ten years? But on the level of the culture as a whole, these individual acts of heroic patience power a society in a hurry, a people who collectively are restlessly innovative. The scientific method gave a formula to follow by which the individually patient and enquiring could push their society forward, and this is precisely what happened with Western civilisation and why Western civilisation advanced so rapidly. If we wish to advance with anything like the rapidity we have previously displayed, we need to make a conscious effort to remember it.

9

CHRISTIANITY

*"It has been often said, very truly, that religion is the
thing that makes the ordinary man feel extraordinary;
it is an equally important truth that religion is the thing
that makes the extraordinary man feel ordinary."*

—G.K.Chesterton, *Charles Dickens: A Critical Study*

WESTERN CIVILISATION WAS BORN IN CLASSICISM,
and grew up in Christianity. For over a thousand years, Christendom was
a term that was synonymous with Western civilisation. For two thousand
years, Christianity has been playing an active role in the identity and politics
of the west, and for most of that period, a dominant role. In Britain, from the
Gregorian mission of 597AD to the present, Christianity has been both an
active and a political presence in England, and utterly dominant culturally
and spiritually from the late 7th century into the 20th century. Still nominally
Christian, most commentators today recognise that we have become a largely
secular society, with much of the population only participating in church
services at the key ceremonies of weddings and funerals. The average British
person today is not a regular churchgoer or an active believer in Christianity,
but we have still to recognise as a culture, honestly and directly, what an
enormous break in our history this contemporary secularism represents.

Nor do we honestly discuss what it means for our society to be truly multi-religious in a fashion not really seen since the 6th century, or how social cohesion and identity functions when millions of our populace are far more actively religious than the host community they have joined, with many adhering to a faith which has a history of animosity and competition with Christianity as long as the history of the existence of Christianity in Britain. We are told by our authorities that even asking such questions is an exercise in prejudice rather than sensible enquiry, and both the Catholic and Protestant churches officially support the view that religious plurality is something to celebrate, with no attendant ill consequences, despite their own sectarian history warning them of the potential dangers.

When Christianity first emerged, few would have predicted the dominant role it would come to assume in Western life, and many of the educated and powerful in particular might have scoffed at the absurd notion that the Roman Empire would both adopt this obscure Jewish sect as its sole state religion and that the insignificant sect would itself outlast the entire structure of Roman power. In some ways, the ascendancy of Christianity was an exact reversal of the template by which the Roman state had subsumed within itself a bewildering multiplicity of faiths without ever damaging the integrity of Roman cultural identity. The Romans had a genius for incorporating the religions of the regions they conquered wholesale, whilst wrapping them in Roman trappings and making them a seamless part of Roman life. Roman pragmatism extended into the spiritual realm, and provided these religions did not threaten the order of the state, the collection of taxes or the acceptance of Roman rule, they were largely left unmolested and intact, with new Roman names but otherwise largely unchanged.

Only two truly significant instances departed from this happy but politically canny pluralism, these being Druidism and Judaism. On conquering Britain, the Romans had already decided that the Druidic faith represented a barbaric threat to good order and productive rule, and tales of the sickening rituals conducted by wild druids were used in exactly the same way that propaganda has always been used to stir nations to action against particularly feared religious groups. Pagan Celtic deities could be incorporated within Roman life by finding some nearly analogous existing Roman divinity and treating the pagan god as a local aspect of that already known quantity, but the druids themselves as a sect were associated with vile practices and potential leaders of rebellion were massacred en masse.

Roman suppression of particularly militant Jewish sects followed a similar pattern. Those that accepted Roman authority were left unmolested; those that incited rebellion were crushed. For the Roman Emperors, right up until Constantine's adoption of the faith, Christianity was just another bewildering offshoot of a primitive monotheistic belief system with a history of insurrectionism. A betting Roman of the 1st century AD might have backed Mithraism, popular with the increasingly politically active legions, to sweep the Empire, or most likely simply have assumed that the pantheism inherited from the beginnings of the state would continue uninterrupted.

Unlike other militant sects of Judaism, however, Christians had the significant advantage of learning from the Roman example and copying those elements which were most effective. It was not only the patronage of Constantine that made the significant difference, but also tactical choices made by the early Christian church and the apostles. In particular, the example of Jesus in making no real distinction between gentile and Jew, and preaching to both, immediately increased the potential of growth for this sect significantly above that of purely Jewish rivals. The sects evidenced in the Dead Sea Scrolls, for example, were never going to proselytise in the manner of the early Christians. (Jewish exclusivity and exceptionalism does, however, have an odd effect in that it makes Jewish integration into other cultures easier. Jews are not going to violently demand that others follow their faith.) But if we also look at the way in which the early Christian church incorporated elements of other faiths in a purely pragmatic fashion, we see, quite ironically, a repetition of Roman methodology.

This is why Christian festivals fall on dates significant to the pagan calendar, and why Christian churches were often built on sites already sacred to pagan gods. Just as Rome had done to the faiths of conquered regions, the conquering Christian church did in turn, allowing the common people to continue almost the same rituals on the same days, simply reconstituted as Christian rather than pagan worship. The more stubbornly resistant local deities could be reconfigured as Christian demons, whilst the more amenable could pass their aspects and holy symbols or dates to some equivalent saint or angel. The fact that many Christian demonic and angelic names end in '–el' is significant, in that this retains the pre-Christian Semitic title 'El', meaning 'god', a title given to various major deities.

Christian theology also had appealing aspects that help explain its success compared to rival faiths of the same period. Many of the cults of the ancient world were mystery sects, requiring a graduated, hierarchical set of devotions. This was, for example, the nature of Mithraism. Even essentially philosophical schools like those of the Pythagoreans followed the structure of a mystery cult in revealing greater truths at successive stages of devotion. Full understanding of these sects might never come for the ordinary follower, and whole classes of humanity (women, slaves, foreigners, etc) might be barred access to even the lowliest levels of initiation. Following Christ's teaching, Christianity did the exact opposite. It offered the same revelations to all and even specifically targeted otherwise despised, lowly or ostracised groups.

Despite some obvious theological misogyny in key myths and teachings (from the guilt of femininity embodied in the roles of Lilith and Eve to the distrust of carnality from St Augustine on), the Christian church did not, for example, exclude women. There is some evidence to suggest that even the exclusion of women from the priesthood was a development not evident in the early Church, and certainly the expectation that priests should be celibate was a later addition rather than a core tenet. It could be said that the patriarchal elements of Christianity derive either from earlier tradition or from the early fathers of the Church, and not from the ministry of Jesus himself.

Christianity, in terms of social issues like class, gender and race, was an unusually welcoming and accommodating faith. Christ ministered to previously despised groups, whether those were lepers or cripples, women or slaves, the prostitute or the destitute. To all of these groups, Christianity offered spiritual enfranchisement, the promise of a reward in heaven based not on social status on Earth, nor even on inculcation in deeper mysteries obtained through long study. Every Christian, regardless of status, received exactly the same promise of redemption and exactly the same promise of eternal happiness hereafter, based only on depth of belief and a willingness to accept Christ. Anyone could become a Christian and anyone could enter the kingdom of heaven. The new faith was first and most enthusiastically embraced by those who had been excluded from serious participation in other faiths.

But this spiritual enfranchisement, this democratisation of the rewards of faith, does not explain the appeal of Christianity to the ruling classes as well as the lowest in society. Christianity spread rapidly from its trivial beginnings and relatively soon encompassed the whole of the Western world, which at that stage meant the whole of the Roman Empire, including North Africa and the Middle East. It spread rapidly in a geographic sense and in terms of dissemination within various strata of society.

Two practical features explain this spread. First, the fact that Christianity always had a missionary, proselytising purpose. The early Christians were not only prepared to travel and spread the word, but expected to do so as a kind of holy mission. The apostles and their immediate followers visited all the major urban centres of the Roman Empire, and successive Popes planned missionary expeditions with all the rigour and care of military expeditions into hostile territory. It is likely that Britain, for example, would not have been converted save for two successive waves of missionary work — the Gregorian mission of 597, followed by the Hiberno-Scottish mission of the 630s. Britain, however, also provides an example of why Constantine chose to adopt Christianity as the sole Roman state religion and why it appealed to the ruling class as much as it appealed to the previously disenfranchised. Again, the example of Christ and how this influenced the development of Christianity as a whole is particularly relevant.

The anticipated Jewish Messiah was specifically a revolutionary figure. He was expected to overturn established hierarchies, and particularly reverse the humiliation of the Roman occupation of Israel. He was a figure of dissent, of civil disorder, of rebellion. He was to be a breaker of chains, a liberator, a bringer of nationalist revival. Most Jewish sects assumed he would be some kind of military leader, or spark an actual, successful revolt against Roman rule. The febrile atmosphere of simmering resentment in the Jewish world towards Roman rule is well described in the works of Josephus, and was just as true throughout Christ's life as during the lives of the apostles in the early Christian church. Certainly, Christ fulfilled this role to a sufficient extent to cause disquiet to the Romans and earn the distrust of the Jewish Sanhedrin, who saw Jesus as a threat to public order. Such incidents as the violent ejection of the moneylenders from the Temple fulfilled this militant and aggressive, subversive role.

But what is perhaps more noteworthy is the extent to which Christ rejected the expected nature of the Messiah. He rejected it first as an exclusively Jewish issue, appealing instead to all mankind. He rejected it secondly in a political sense, by being a persuader rather than an agitator. The moments in which Christ becomes enraged are far rarer than the moments in which he is moved to compassion. He can describe himself as a sword, but more commonly as a shepherd, a protector rather than a conqueror. His miracles are exclusively compassionate and merciful rather than violent and disruptive. He does not curse his enemies with madness or plagues or bring down the walls of opposing cities, as prior prophets were wont to do. He does not drown a pursuing army, but lets himself be captured by a handful of soldiers. He does not lead a Jewish rebellion, but rebels against Jewish authorities rather than reject the divine truth of his own nature. He does not destroy Roman power, but tells his followers to render unto Caesar that which belongs to Caesar. And the summation of his message, the most extensive and complete recitation of his system of belief, comes in the Sermon on the Mount, where we are told that the meek shall inherit the earth, not the militant. Just as the New Testament as a whole reveals a more moderate God than the Old, so too is Christ himself a less revolutionary figure than anticipated.

Christian theology, as it developed following Christ's example in the period before its adoption by Constantine, became increasingly less threatening to the social order and in particular to the ruling class, whether that was the remaining authorities of Rome or the pagan kings who followed. In the time of Nero, Christianity was viewed almost as a terrorist group would be viewed today, and Nero's persecutions began with the false assumption or cynical propagandistic lie that the Great Fire was initiated deliberately by Christian fanatics. Every Emperor who persecuted the early Christians saw Christianity in a similar light — as an insurrectionist, dangerous movement, a criminal faith sure to disrupt social harmony.

As with all faiths, particularly young ones, this fear could be true, and the early history of Christianity, especially in the period where it definitively supplanted paganism, had its fair share of violent mobs, such as the one led by Peter the Lector in 415/16AD, which murdered Hypatia in Alexandria. But violent strains of Christianity, whilst they have always existed, are a contradiction of the teaching of the founding prophet of the faith, rather than a continuation of his teaching. This is in stark contrast to Islam, of course, where the most violent practitioners of that faith, the most rapacious, cruel and domineering fanatics, are the ones most closely following the example found in the life of Mohammed.

What Constantine realised, and what subsequent pagan kings also realised, was that in addressing itself to the dispossessed and the lowly, whilst also preaching a doctrine of acceptance, forgiveness and rewards to follow that were spiritual rather than material, Christianity could actually serve as a potent means of mitigating against social disorder and civil disturbance. Far from being a secretive cult inspiring acts of rebellion, an open and officially condoned Christianity offered a form of hope and comfort that might accommodate lowlier rungs of society quietly going about their business without ever seeking to overthrow the established order. For if the concerns of the earthly realm are fleeting, and the rewards of heaven eternal, then obedience in the temporary vale of tears that is life is easier to accept.

Christianity therefore appealed to rulers in the same way, perversely, that it appealed to the most despised elements of society. It provided the comfort of anticipated reward to the latter, and the comfort of delayed rebellion to the former. Many centuries later, slave owners would encourage their slaves to develop Christian sentiments for the same mixture of cynical and spiritual reasons. Spreading the faith was part of any Christian's duty, and would save the soul of the individual converted or convinced whilst marking a positive in the ledger of the converter's earthly deeds. But it could also be used to justify and enhance an unequal social system. Constantine adopted Christianity precisely because of Christ's rejection of military rebellion and acceptance of earthly authorities having a place and purpose separate to the spiritual quest of Christian self-development.

So what we see in Christianity is a faith that appealed to both the ruled and, somewhat later but just as powerfully, to those who ruled. The Great Chain of Being and the passive elements of Christianity offered those in power a narrative with which to quell dissent and a sacred endorsement of their power. A Christian king, like Constantine, acquired a powerful, opinion-forming ally in the form of an educated priesthood which increasingly proselytised on behalf of converted rulers as well as on behalf of the Church itself. Priests supplied organisation, education, and propaganda to rulers who had few viable alternative options when looking for candidates suitable for filling these roles. A mystery cult in the ancient world oftentimes combined spiritual exclusivity with political militancy. Being both secretive and disruptive, such cults were often a nuisance to established authority. Christianity, by contrast, when allied to and directed by a ruling class, offered spiritual enfranchisement in return for political harmony.

Those who have a particular grudge towards or distaste for Christianity will of course regard this political harmony as a negative, seeing it as purely a means by which the powerful give a sacred veneer to their greed and exploitation. These are the respondents who are most likely to cite the way in which, for example, European and American slave owners justified slavery by reference to Biblical tales, or point out how Christians conducted atrocities during the Crusades or engaged in conquest and suppression during the colonial era. Like Marx, they might view religion as the opium of the masses, seeing it solely as a kind of drug to still dissent, to cloud minds and preserve baseless traditions. Others have objected to the passivity of Christianity, with Gibbon seeing it as a drain on the purpose and self-belief of Rome, since increasing numbers of the people who might otherwise have contributed towards society were drawn instead towards internal reflection and ascetic retreat.

Nietzsche gave perhaps the most sustained and passionate rejection of this pacifying aspect of Christianity, seeing it as an effete and useless betrayal of the will to power that underlies all human achievement. Others, conversely, will point to the many sectarian religious conflicts within Christianity, from the Thirty Years War, to the French Wars of Religion, even into the twentieth century and the Troubles in Northern Ireland. They will point to Christian killers and Christian cults, to Waco and to wackos, and assert that these indicate that Christianity is just as irrational and violent as any other faith.

The people doing this of course, knowingly or unknowingly, will be Cultural Marxists. They will not genuinely be inheritors of the kind of reasoned critique Gibbon offered, nor will they be philosophical followers of Nietzsche. They will simply be looking for tools with which to undermine the centrality of Christianity in the history and nature of the West, as part of their devoted project of destroying all that Western civilisation is. They will not acknowledge, for example, that Christianity was founded on the rejection of violent solutions, not the expression of them. They will not recognise the huge gulf in personal example between the behaviour of Christ and the behaviour of Mohammed. They will not recognise that the New Testament represents a revision and an evolution away from the jealous, angry, psychopathic God presented to us in the Old Testament, nor that every significant religious conflict within Christian countries resulted in yet further moves away from Western society regarding religiously motivated violence as acceptable or necessary.

They will not even act as if the secular transformation that occurred from the crisis of faith in the late nineteenth century onwards is a reality, but will pretend that Christianity yet retains a pre-eminence that must be challenged. They will cite the Crusades not because they have any special interest in or knowledge of that period, but because that period is replete with Christians acting contrary to Christian teaching. The fact that the Judeo-Christian tradition gave us, in effect, our first truly articulate conception of human rights in the form of the Ten Commandments is ignored. The limits set on what we may or may not do to others and the sins presented as sin within the Christian tradition still offer a moral framework that underpins our entire conception of good and evil. Most of the secular modern populace today within Western societies base even their rejection of extremist religion on solid foundations of Christian history and morality.

Cultural Marxists, by contrast, despise Christianity precisely because it has, over two thousand years, become woven firmly into the tapestry of Western identity. GK Chesterton pointed out that in the absence of God — by which he effectively meant the absence of Christianity — it is not the case that the people believe in nothing. Actually, the removal of the centrality of Christian faith in our lives paves the way for allowing the people to believe in anything, including far more extreme and violent belief systems. This is why Communism is an anti-religious movement, because, of course, religion competes directly with Communism in shaping mental attitudes and social responses. Communism does not want a coherent or powerful rival for the minds of the people and the destiny of society. Both Nazism and Communism are predicated on the weakness and decline of Christianity, whilst the spread of Islam in Western society is facilitated by the lack of a strong spiritual belief system ready to oppose its spread.

The Western nations that retain a strong sense of Christendom and Christian identity are the ones which have been most effective in resisting Islamisation. Nations such as Poland or Hungary stood at the frontline of Christendom in all the centuries during which powerful Muslim nations, such as the Ottoman Empire, threatened it. They recall this history and identity in ways that more complacent and removed, still nominally fellow Christian countries do not. This is why Viktor Orbán, the Hungarian Prime Minister, can speak about defending Western civilisation unapologetically, knowing exactly what that means, knowing the centrality of Christian identity within the shared cultural heritage of the West and knowing, too, just what it would mean to fully jettison that inheritance.

In Britain we are surrounded by the evidence of that centrality, and daily deny its reality. England was knit together by Christianity. Every parish, every stone Norman church, every cathedral, is the tale of England's spirituality. In Alfred the Great, English nationalism and Christian piety cohere, making the one almost impossible to feel and understand without reference to the other. At one point, every school day opened and closed with Christian prayer and reflection. In the English Gothic, we had our own unique architecture to provide a physical testament to the soaring ambition of our spiritual life. The English church was the hub of the village and town, the place where agreements were made and kept, where lives were recorded and lived, where the passage of unrelenting time was soothed by the contemplation of timeless verities.

It is impossible now to conceive of an England that is England without the Norman church, where brutal conquest was mitigated by shared belief and where Norman and Saxon alike worked towards building a shared identity of inviolable strength which lasted a thousand uninterrupted years. In English choral music, we have a rich store of profoundly moving musical accomplishment almost entirely unknown by the descendants of those who created it. In Christian hymns, we had a shared lexicon of feeling and expression which gave meaningful connection to the past and meaningful hope to the future. In English field and country churchyard, the bones of our ancestors reposed, sheltered in sanctity as much as soil. Through wars and tribulations, the Christian faith both guided and comforted us, an ever-present unchanging point of reference as vital to the Edwardian as it was to the Elizabethan. The uniquely English compromise of the Elizabethan religious settlement expressed a national genius for largely avoiding the devastating internal conflicts of pure religious hatred that gripped continental Europe. Any Western nationalist or traditionalist, regardless of his or her own spiritual choices and personal belief, must accept and honour the importance of Christianity in the story of Western civilisation.

It is a sad thing today to see the extent to which Christianity is reduced and deliberately targeted by Cultural Marxists for utter annihilation, including by those within Christian churches, often in the most senior positions of authority within the clerical hierarchy. The Church of England, for example, today produces few real believers in the message of Christ, and many of the supine, passive, enfeebled weaklings that Nietzsche railed against. Christ's rejection of militancy was not that of a weak man, and certainly not that of a person unsure of his own beliefs. Christian martyrs never refused to speak out against injustice or the suppression of their faith in the way that contemporary Christian leaders do. Enter any Christian church in England, save for the evangelical churches of some immigrant communities, and you will see a dying faith in the empty pews and cold, neglected spaces. Attend a funeral and note how few voices are raised when the hymns are sung, or how little the words are remembered.

Do the leaders of the Church note these changes? Do they give any indication of concern about them? Do they lament when Christianity is routinely mocked, and do they actively engage in promoting Christian interests? Do they speak out about the global extinction of ancient Christian communities by advancing Islam, or oppose the spread of mosques within their own supposedly Christian nations? Of course not. Rather, they celebrate and aid this cultural replacement. They invite Muslims to preach in Christian churches and repeat the bland, blind platitudes of contemporary liberalism. They concern themselves with leftist causes and shibboleths whilst their own faith withers away. The people reject them, because nobody believes in those who do not believe in themselves. Church attendance has almost passed a critical point where recovery is impossible, and in doing so has robbed the English people of meaningful community. Our isolated lives are ones in which all of the things which bound us together are unravelled, and the decline of the Christian church is a key part of that.

10

CAPITALISM

*"The inherent vice of capitalism is the unequal sharing of blessings;
the inherent vice of socialism is the equal sharing of misery."*

—Winston Churchill

THE MODERN WORLD IS DOMINATED BY THE
economic system of capitalism. Human beings of all political persuasions
live in the reality of the complete domination of capitalism and its triumph
over all alternative systems of economic and social order. The only significant
threats to capitalism, the only real alternatives to have arisen in the last two
centuries or more, have been Nazism and Communism, the first of which
reached an active accommodation with capitalist plutocracy after the Night
of the Long Knives and the purging of the most socialist elements of the
Nazi Party, and the second of which was thoroughly defeated in its Russian
birthplace and now accommodates capitalism in a very similar fashion to
Nazi Germany in its sole remaining significant enclave of China.

Socialist governments in northern Europe which are held to be examples
of the ability of non-capitalist systems to function without terror, repression
or economic decline are of course merely capitalist nations with a socialist
veneer in the form of a significant welfare state. There is nowhere except
perhaps in the most war-torn, socially fragmented, chaotic wildernesses of

the earth where capitalism is not the dominant mode of exchange. A few remaining indigenous and isolated populations may still depend on barter, but even these are ever further encroached by the voracious advance of neighbouring capitalist societies.

The triumph of Western civilisation was first and foremost an economic triumph. The Agricultural and Industrial Revolutions were as significant markers in the inevitable rise of the West as any military prowess, perhaps considerably more significant regardless of the genius of individual battlefield commanders. French and British colonial expansion and competition in the 18th and 19th century was the most obvious illustration of the economic roots of both Western success and its internal rivalries. The battle for Empire was a battle to control trade routes, dominate manufacturing, economically outperform near rivals and capture markets. Generals win battles, but economies win wars, and it is also economic realities which largely decide where and when wars occur. We can see examples of this throughout Western history, from Rome's subdual of Carthage or Egypt, which both possessed strong economic as well as social or military motivations, through to the pivotal role played by the Venetian Republic in the decline of Constantinople.

As feudal societies gave way to proto-capitalist ones, the economic underpinnings of the causes of conflict only increased in significance. The British gained an enormous edge based on their early Industrial Revolution, and any subsequent power that wished to challenge them had to adopt the same economic framework and deliver the same kind of industrial might. Britain's naval- and trade-based Empire as we have earlier described followed the Athenian model of hegemony, but there was also something Roman in the engineering and technical genius displayed by post-industrial Britain in its swift march to superpower status. This dominance could only be challenged once other nations possessed the same kind of industrial might, together with equal or greater control of dependent markets of a greater size. This is what was occurring with Germany immediately prior to WWI and what did occur with the US during WWI and WWII. In the aftermath of the first of these conflicts, the world realised how dependent it had become on the US economy succeeding, whilst in the aftermath of the second, it realised that even the UK had become a dependent and subordinate client market of the US. The delay in the US entering each war, together with the unlocking of the enormous economic potential of its size and populace by supplying the needs of other economies during conflict, shifted the economic and therefore military and cultural power from the UK to the US.

In our own time, two potentially seismic shifts of both power and perception are occurring. Despite the rise of the US and USSR as global superpowers in the 20th century and their stand off during the Cold War, European ascendancy, compared to that of other regions, largely continued unchallenged. Whilst the old Empires shrivelled and died, the mass of European and North American citizens enjoyed considerably better economic conditions than the remainder of the planet, barring a Japan which, post-war, had exactly mirrored the route to success of previous Western economies. Japanese and, to a lesser extent, Taiwanese economic success was predicated not on a radical departure from the Western template of capitalist success but a faithful mirroring of it, stripped of the colonialist dimensions which had proven so disastrously misguided when attempted by Japan before and during WWII.

The Japanese economic miracle of the 1950s and 1960s depended on copying Western models, but doing the same things more cheaply, quickly and efficiently. Whilst a zaibatsu might possess a uniquely Japanese feel, it was not really until the 1980s that any sense of this registering a challenge to the continuing cultural hegemony of Western civilisation could be found within Western popular culture. Suddenly at that point, cyberpunk novelists like William Gibson, in *Neuromancer* (1984), were envisaging futures shaped by Japanese styles and Japanese attitudes, whilst the same aesthetic (not present in Philip K.Dick's novel) famously informed Ridley Scott's panoramic vision in the original *Bladerunner*. Pulpish action films like *Black Rain* (1989) and *Rising Sun* (1993) suggested an undercurrent of US unease at Japanese economic prowess, perhaps linked to the scale of US indebtedness and the amount of this debt that was held by the Japanese government, banks and institutions, together with increasingly visible Japanese investment abroad. This Japanese false dawn, however, followed by a long economic stagnation, was only a ripple compared to the threat today posed by Chinese adoption of and success at the capitalist model, particularly as, unlike Japan, that advance is linked to an officially Communist one-party political system and an enormous military infrastructure. Western unease at this advance does not need to be presented in fictive forms through action movies, but is front and centre of contemporary political policy and has entered a direct stage of tariff competition under Trump's presidency.

During the Cold War there were few points at which Soviet Communism could have been considered to present a cultural or economic challenge. The threat of imminent mutually assured nuclear destruction was of course a psychological shadow of no insignificant dimension, but in a strange way, the totality of such a possibility rendered it less real than more prosaic economic competition. Those who genuinely feared such a possibility beyond the 1960s were increasingly a minority, eventually becoming a fringe movement of activists in organisations like Campaign for Nuclear Disarmament (CND). By the time that a member of CND became the leader of the Labour Party, membership of such a group had become almost a comical gesture, identifying those who were members with the furthest and most ridiculous extremes of non-serious student politics.

Even when Reagan was calling the USSR the 'evil empire', the signs of its imminent collapse were discernible insofar as the threat it posed was no longer viewed in any existential fashion. Culturally, everyone was aware that Soviet youth was listening to Western music, mimicking Western styles, watching Western films and dreaming of escape to the West whilst a long succession of increasingly aged and decrepit dictators were powerless to prevent it. By the 1980s, it appeared as if Western civilisation in its modern incarnation of consumerism, self-expression and self-confident capitalism could not be challenged. The disasters of Communism — the number of deaths, the economic failure, the poor living standards, the lack of basic rights or commodities, the empty shelves and the unpaid workers, were obvious. The only serious rival to Western capitalism for much of the 20th century was a moribund corpse. At the same time, British decline had been reversed by Thatcherite policies to such an extent that it was even capable of both wanting to fight and being able to win an essentially colonial conflict in the Falklands.

These issues might seem removed from the topic of pure capitalism, were it not for the strong connection between cultural confidence and economic success. Each feeds the other. Markets thrive and economies boom when consumers feel confident, whilst economic success powers the spread of cultural influence as the national or local products associated with that success acquire an additional patina of desirability. People desire an association with success rather than failure, and confidence can become an economically self-fulfilling prophecy (obviously, if this confidence has no tether to reality, it presages a moment of devastating realisation first seen with the South Sea Bubble). In the 1980s, it had already become obvious — to both sides of the conflict — who had won the battle of cultures between the capitalist West and the Soviet East, The fall of the Berlin Wall was as certain as the defeat of Ivan Drago. Perhaps the only people who were surprised were the Western liberal intelligentsia, who had already established a long and ignoble tradition of betting on the other side. And it is to this class, together with the most perceptive of the late Soviet agents, that we owe the existence of Cultural Marxism, identity politics and the fact that the triumph of Western civilisation over its last remaining opponent was so swiftly followed by a crisis of confidence rather than a renewed flowering of intent.

Between the 19th century and the current day, capitalism has fundamentally reconfigured the world. Western civilisation, by spreading capitalism, democracy and the keys to its own success to others, has significantly extended the average human lifespan and improved the average conditions under which all human beings live. Contemporary populations today enjoy lifestyles that medieval monarchs, in many ways, could not emulate and would perhaps envy. Via an inoculation or a simple antibiotic, people can survive illnesses or surgeries that would once have crippled or killed them. We are surrounded by technological marvels that allow us access to entertainment at any hour of the day or night. We can communicate instantaneously with people on any part of the globe. We can access the entire store of human knowledge more readily than any previous generation. We can immerse ourselves in artificial lives or fictional universes without even the effort required of reading a book.

In 1820, 90% of the world's population lived in absolute poverty, and despite adding billions to that population, today less than 20% do so. We measure poverty in relative terms and cite as poverty-stricken those who possess more than kings of the ancient world owned. Of course, we still have people who are homeless or penniless, but they are far more of an exception than they would have been in previous eras. In the first world, we can identity our poorest by medical conditions caused by obesity, rather than those caused by starvation.

By contrast, the most recently offered alternatives to Western capitalism have enacted deliberate famines resulting in millions of deaths. They have denied basic human rights, they have imprisoned and executed political dissidents and entirely innocent victims. They have formed societies characterised by torture and repression, and in post-colonial Africa, for example, have engaged regularly in barbarities against their own and neighbouring populations. In South America, we have seen countless examples of dictatorial regimes, of both the left and the right, almost always inflicting economic collapse and terrible conditions of existence, first on their political opponents, but soon on their entire populace. Communist and hard-left socialist regimes globally, from Cuba to China and from Venezuela to Vietnam, have been responsible for 100 million unnecessary deaths in little over a century. The full roll call of shame is minutely and accurately recorded, according to the best academic methodology by leading scholars, in The Black Book of Communism. Any student can obtain this book quite readily from online bookshops or from a public library, or access a summary of its contents in seconds after a Google search.

One would think, given this and given the triumph of the West in facing down first the horrors of Nazism and then the Soviet menace in relatively recent history, that it would be almost embarrassing for anyone to question either the benefits of capitalism or the positives of recurrent and identifying features of Western civilisation such as universal enfranchisement, women's rights, gay rights, minority rights, human rights generally, the rule of law, the freedom of the press, the separation of Church and State, the freedom of religious association and the continually improving standards of living enjoyed by every stratum of society. One would think that those who question capitalism by preferring the murderous system of Communism, or who concentrate solely on ancient evils enacted by the West rather than the obvious and pervasive advantages of Western civilisation, would be considered the most bizarre of wilfully obtuse extremists, odd absurdists banished to the fringes of society. This is not, of course, the case. Today, there are millions of people within the West who support alternatives to Western civilisation or who actively work against it. These include left-leaning intellectuals, anarchists, Communists and jihadists. Their opposition ranges from frequently expressed scorn and contempt all the way through to active terrorism, but they are united in despising the history, culture and peoples of the West and in working in opposition to their interests.

It is at this point that we should consider the nature of this opposition to Western civilisation as a whole. The first point to acknowledge is that it is not a process directed by any one individual or any one organisation. The second is that it unites extremely disparate groups whose ideological positions would be anathema to each other were it not for their shared and greater hatred of Western civilisation. The third point is that most of these groups would not be able to function without having already established themselves in positions of leadership within the very nation states and infrastructures to which they are virulently opposed, and without using the benevolent features of Western civilisation to their own advantage.

Other than repressive methodologies, the only characteristic some of these groups share is their fundamental(ist) and intense loathing of Western society, Western history, Western people and Western nations. But ironically, this intense hatred of the West often coordinates their actions more effectively than any defence the West has managed in response, and creates campaigns of cultural destruction more effective in their multiplicity than they would be as a coordinated conspiracy. And since capitalism is an amoral system of exchange that rewards the supply of what people want more than it rewards any inherent virtue, so long as there is a market for ideas inimical to Western civilisation, there will also be a profit in such ideas.

There are influential individuals who embody these contradictions within Cultural Marxism. George Soros, the Hungarian-born billionaire who has become a key hate figure for the Right, is both an arch-capitalist and a radical progressive Cultural Marxist. His international meddling and 'philanthropic' support of leftist political causes can lead defenders of Western civilisation into the trap of adopting a 'conspiracy theory' view of Cultural Marxism. But reducing this cultural phenomenon to the agency of a single individual renders a genuine concern at the decline of the West faintly ridiculous because it repeats purely fictive tropes (like that of the Bond supervillain) which, rationally, we all know to be simplistic and false. We all know that major cultural shifts can be hugely influenced by individuals but are not solely about individuals. To pretend that they are, that every example of Cultural Marxism represents the callous hand of George Soros, allows other Cultural Marxists an easy route to mocking and denying the profound truth of their shared culpability in our cultural collapse.

This is not to deny that Soros is an enemy of Western civilisation and Western nations. He is. But he is not some spider at the centre of a web responsible for every tremor of every strand of Cultural Marxism as a whole. His financial support for organisations which promote mass immigration or thought-control legislation or open borders or identity politics or any of the other poisons which are offered as medicines is enormously destructive, as is his purely selfish financial speculation ('The Man Who Broke the Bank of England') that acquired the resources he deploys in the first place. But George Soros did not invent the ideology he follows, nor has he ever been alone in promoting it.

Soros is also representative of an international business class which is almost entirely globalist in outlook. This class sees the nation state as a barrier to its power and to the things it believes in. Some individuals of this class cynically support open borders, for example, simply because they facilitate their own business models, because they provide ready access to cheap labour regardless of national boundaries. Some others are as giddily idealistic and misguided as Hollywood starlets or Corbyn-supporting students, and have a Gene Roddenberry future of frictionless, borderless utopia in mind whereby all human conflict magically dissolves once nation states no longer exist or when international organisations entirely replace them. Both the most aggressive wealth- and power-driven cynic and the most committed ignorant child can support a Cultural Marxist agenda for their own entirely contradictory reasons, which is why, for example, we see Big Business and student radicals united in distaste for nationalist populism.

Soros is perhaps unusual in the extent to which he unites within his own character both the cynical and the idealistic. He has spoken, for example, about never letting morality intrude on his business decisions and never thinking about the consequences of those decisions for others. In a now notorious '60 Minutes' interview, he even agreed that he felt no guilt for participating in the seizure of Jewish property and goods during the Nazi occupation of Hungary. At the same time, it is obvious that he regards his support for leftist causes as a moral crusade and has a moral objection to nationalism. He is probably entirely sincere in the sense of regarding the causes he funds as being 'good', despite the actual damage they do.

Support for capitalism as a whole is not an endorsement of any individual capitalist or a moral judgement on every capitalist action. You can support the system of international financial transaction that allows a Soros to exist whilst lamenting what Soros has done with the proceeds from the system that allowed him to become rich. There is a very trite and easy moral argument to be made against capitalism. This argument is usually made by citing the worst capitalists as if they were the 'true face' of capitalism as a whole: the behaviour of nineteenth century robber barons, for example, or the companies that used slave labour in Nazi Germany or Imperial Japan, or slavery itself by which human beings were reduced to the status of disposable commodities, or the pollution and ecological consequence that has derived from oil and logging companies.

Another shortcut to condemnation is to be found in the unequal distribution of resources inherent to capitalist systems, with critics pointing out, for example, the tiny pittances on which third-world populations depend compared to first-world populations. All of these criticisms, like the best lies, are partly true. Of course, to any rational person, the rapid exhaustion of our natural resources and the despoilment of the planet is a concern. Of course, to any rational person, pointing to a Rupert Murdoch figure, or more recently a Philip Green, for example, will suggest that untrammelled individual capitalist endeavour can be a deeply negative thing. Even those who are relatively benign, but rewarded far in excess of any apparent skill or talent, or any inherent worth above that of others, can suggest the moral flaws of capitalism. Reality television, for example, has both produced many such individuals and made us all more aware of them than we would necessarily like to be.

But all of these criticisms are based on the fundamental misapprehension that the economic system under which we live has some inherent duty to result in entirely equal outcomes. It mistakes the purpose of these economic systems whilst simultaneously ignoring the many benefits of the least worst of our choices and the far greater excesses of the only sustained alternatives that have ever been offered. Capitalism is not equal. It is not fair. It is not just. But it works, and in the process of working offers the best hope of fairness and justice we can reach. Under capitalism, anyone has a chance of reaching their full human potential or of enjoying the level of material success they aspire to, even if that chance is more remote for some than for others. Under capitalism, millions of people are likely to be dissatisfied with their lot in life but, crucially, they are also both more likely to be alive in the first place and more likely to have a chance to change the things that irk them. Life, liberty and the pursuit of happiness are all more possible under capitalism than under communism, and the founding fathers of the US were wise in offering only the pursuit of happiness rather than the guarantee of it. Capitalism does not give the guarantee it knows cannot, for everyone, be fulfilled. Communism and other utopian ideologies do, and do so dishonestly.

Much of the distaste for capitalism evident in the West today revolves around the concept of fairness. It is considered unfair that some have more than others. We are supposed to be determined to make our societies fairer, and the means of doing so are supposed to come via interventions by the State in the form of taxation or other means of duress. This is all well and good provided you don't trouble yourself to think about what real fairness might be and simply assume that equality of outcome represents fairness. But in order to artificially enforce an equality of outcome, one must be unfair when it comes to equality of opportunity. This is what 'positive discrimination' and social engineering methods do — supplant one form of unfairness for another, claiming that an unfairness which derives from natural causes or from the accepted interactions of a capitalist system is somehow more unfair than the unfairness which derives from government intervention backed by force.

Anyone familiar with the behaviour of governments and their agents might be forgiven for preferring to trust market forces of capitalist exchange rather than utopian interventions by government fiat. The expectation that an economic system should be 'fair', and the idea that fairness is easily determined by governments, is a form of thinking that ironically can only arise amongst those who have generally benefited from the kind of comfortable existence a successful capitalist nation provides. Those who have lived within Communist systems where the State decides both what is fair and how goods are to be distributed soon realise that an amoral market is less malevolent than an immoral government.

It may be unfair, for example, that some by mere happenstance of birth inherit greater opportunities than others. But there is a logical distinction between, say, the inheritance of property and the ability to retain what previous generations have acquired, and the use of nepotistic contacts to secure special social advantages or particularly good jobs. If another person is born to wealthy parents, that wealth has not been denied to me by being theirs; it has not been taken from me. But if their parent gets them a job for which I am better qualified and prepared to interview for, then it could indeed be said that their success comes at my expense. Wealth can also be created by supplying a need, without that wealth being taken unwillingly from others. Thus it might be unequal that the founder of a business or the inventor of a product or a singer or sportsperson is far richer than I am, but none of it came at my expense or by limiting my chances. If society values the skills possessed by another more than the skills I possess, that is unfortunate for me and results in unequal outcomes, but it is not necessarily unjust. I have the option of acquiring those skills or supplying something else which is valued as well.

It is when we look at the alternatives to capitalist exchange that we see a far better picture of whether this is the least fair or most fair system available to us. Under feudalism, some social classes in almost their entirety will be permanently locked out of the kind of possibilities capitalism provides. The society as a whole will be more stagnant and any advance or growth more hesitant, as it is denied the engine of entrepreneurship, innovation and rapid wealth creation that capitalism comes fitted with. Pre-feudal societies, hunter-gatherers, nomadic herders or very early settled agrarian societies will not have the specialisation and inbuilt incentives that power rapid advance. If you want a society to remain unchanged for thousands of years, they are a better choice than capitalism, but if you want advancement, civilisation and technological progress, they are not. Social attitudes will be just as stagnant in pre-capitalist societies as the technological progress displayed by these cultures.

And what of communism, the only significant alternative to capitalism that is still extant? We have already noted the tendency of this system towards a scale of evil far in excess of capitalism. Capitalism can be deeply unjust. It can be morally dubious. But it is not required to be. The best capitalist exchanges are willing ones. The most efficiently functioning capitalist endeavours do not destroy the market they depend upon. Total exploitation ends all potential future profit. Treating customers as a locust treats a field will not ensure long-term profitability.

Communism, by contrast, requires the use of force. Since the distribution of wealth and power is always unequal, to enforce equality requires the use of power. Nobody accepts the seizure of his or her goods without complaint. Someone must use force to allow such redistribution, and what this also means is that the agents of redistribution immediately become a new class of more obvious exploiters than those they supplant. Human nature means it is impossible for a group, the political class of active Communist party members, to acquire redistributive power without it being used to their own advancement. You replace businessmen or capitalists who make a profit from your willing exchanges with bureaucrats and officials who gain an advantage from your oppression. And the very process of moving from capitalism to communism in a manner which requires violence means that the social bars and restraints on the behaviour of individual capitalists do not exist in the case of individual communists. Society has already abandoned whatever legal or moral restraints existed prior to the Communist takeover. Moreover, to keep an excuse for the new distribution, to justify its own power, a Communist state can never 'end the Revolution' but must continually discover, rediscover and invent enemies which explain its own depravities and failings.

To keep control of the means of production and the outcomes of distribution, the Communist state must, in effect, keep killing and sustaining the secret police infrastructure, purges, gulags, death camps, etc. that allow it to rule through fear. Capitalism can rule through incentive or hope, through the possibility of individual advancement; Communism, except to a minority who might find the apparatus of grim power itself attractive (the Beria-type sadist keen for opportunities to rape and torture), cannot offer many inducements. It therefore must deploy terror.

To give a broader understanding of why, despite so obviously offering many more personal and social benefits than the alternatives, capitalism is increasingly unpopular, we must recognise two things. First, globalism has created a form of capitalism that is more rapacious than capitalism in general has been for at least a century. As the power of nation states wanes, the international capitalist pays less and less attention to the needs and concerns of the populace in any particular locale. And that populace are well aware of the fact. Corporatism, the corrupt influence of monopoly multinationals, is more active today than a healthy capitalist competition, darkening perceptions of capitalism as a whole just as the behaviour of a football hooligan taints the image of an entire football club. The working class of the US or the UK are well aware that these larger, predatory forms of capitalism do not have their best interests at heart.

Second, in a society in which the greatest resource, power and wealth is already concentrated amongst those who, through tainted education systems, have become Cultural Marxists, it becomes profitable to be overtly political, and political in ways directly contrary to the interests of the majority. Companies will start to abandon the idea of maximising profit by appealing to the majority of consumers, and replace it with the idea of maximising profit by appealing to consumers who possess the majority of wealth. This is what is occurring with the grotesque spectacle of 'woke capitalism', where companies like Nike, Gillette, Starbucks or Ben & Jerry's look to increase their profits by joining in and leading attacks on the working class majority, or on men or on white people (or all three). The same phenomenon has occurred with major entertainment industry corporations like Marvel and Disney. Once apolitical franchises, or harmlessly idealistic ones like Star Trek, become vehicles of 'progressive' values on the assumption that any revenue lost from a disgruntled general populace is compensated and exceeded by the revenue gained from the delighted middle and upper class.

Third, and finally, there is an inherent weakness in pure capitalism, even at its most beneficial. All human needs, fundamentally, fall into one of two categories. They are either the needs of the body or the needs of the mind; they are either about comfort or about meaning. Our most basic needs are those of the body. We must have sustenance. We must have shelter. We must have safety. Capitalism is a superb system for meeting these needs of the body with the greatest frequency, for the greatest number of people. But no human being is truly made content just by meeting these basic requirements, nor is their contentment assured by adding more and more material possessions, by opportunities to shop, by ready availability of goods, or by personal wealth and luxury. For no matter how comfortable our existence becomes, the mind craves a different sustenance to the body. Our minds, what the more religiously minded might call our 'souls' or 'spirits', require meaning. Only ideas can feed this hunger, only belief can assuage this need. Religions speak to the needs of the mind, no matter how idiotic their beliefs might be. Nationalism does too. These are the kinds of needs covered by our understanding of our identity, and politics itself might be seen as the art of balancing these needs within a social context.

What the modern world lacks is meaning. Creeds like Cultural Marxism or Islam supply that need, no matter how evil or illogical or just plain stupid the answers they give might be. Consumerism does not feed the need for meaning. It can soothe the body, but never satisfy the mind. When capitalism thrived in a Christian context, this was not a concern that would ever damage capitalism itself. The body was made more comfortable by capitalism, and the mind could be soothed by Christian meaning. But our society has removed the meaning of God and the meaning of the nation, and alternatives, far more damaging ones, fill that void as we speak. Alien gods and a religion of self-loathing fill the space vacated by Christianity, a space capitalism was never designed to fill.

11

A Communist Conspiracy

"The years ahead will be great ones for our country, for the cause of freedom and the spread of civilization. The West will not contain Communism, it will transcend Communism. We will not bother to denounce it, we'll dismiss it as a sad, bizarre chapter in human history whose last pages are even now being written."

—Ronald Reagan

In 1984, G. Edward Griffin conducted a lengthy interview with ex-KGB officer and Soviet defector, Yuri Bezmonov. In the dying days of the Soviet Union, but at a point where imminent collapse was still not obvious to all, Bezmonov explained the Soviet propaganda techniques which aimed to undermine Western civilisation and the reasoning behind them, as well as the notable effects such propaganda had achieved. The full interview is available on Youtube and is highly relevant to the central topic of this book, which is the contrast between Western civilisation and the Cultural Marxist movements that despise our history, culture and people.

Bezmonov's argument was that many of the internal divisions and dissensions within Western culture were not accidental, nor was the growth of these tensions and their societal impacts. Western students, for example, did not engage in radical politics and extreme leftwing theories accidentally, but because they were guided towards these things by deliberate intent, essentially via Soviet propaganda directed by KGB allies. The 'useful idiots' of the Western intelligentsia, as Lenin described them, had been purposely recruited by KGB agents to spread the kind of disinformation, self-hatred and self-critical ideas which collectively defined radical opposition to Western society.

In terms of the educational establishment in the US and in major Western nations like the UK, this argument is more convincing than it might initially appear. The post-war period after 1945 saw history teaching and related humanities subjects dominated by historians who saw their main purpose as explaining the inherent flaws and contradictions of Western societies. The key formers of the overall trend of history teaching were a school of historians who described themselves as Marxists. Eric Hobsbawm shaped history teaching in the UK, for example, more than any other single historian, but was also politically engaged, active in both the Labour Party and in more radically socialist and communist movements. Hobsbawn was once asked if the millions of deaths resulting from communism were an acceptable price to pay for the socialist utopia he awaited. He replied in the affirmative and moreover stated that, essentially, he would set no upper limit on the number of deaths acceptable to create such a 'perfect' society.

Despite such chilling and, some might say psychopathic views, Hobsbawm was not a figure removed from the mainstream of academia. A figure like David Irving, who questioned the Holocaust and praised certain aspects of fascism and Nazism, was, no doubt rightly, considered beyond the academic pale, but scores of historians who conducted the same kind of apologia on behalf of murderous communism were never considered outside the academic mainstream and helped to shape a society in which support for communism is not greeted with the same horror as support for Nazism. When Hobsbawn died, his funeral was attended by many of the great and the good from supposedly mainstream political parties of the liberal left, by people who had occupied high offices of state and by people who aspired to do so in future. He had been a close personal friend of the father of future Labour leader Ed Miliband, but when these links were pointed out alongside some of Hobsbawm's unsavoury and totalitarian views by a British tabloid newspaper, it was the newspaper which received widespread criticism and not the tacit advocates and apologists for communist regimes.

One has only to imagine the different reactions that would arise were a right-wing politician to attend the funeral of a David Irving figure to realise the entirely different standards applied to academic support for past tyrannies, depending on whether those tyrannies are left-wing or right-wing in nature. One also requires only a cursory knowledge of the likes of Philby and the rest of the Cambridge Five to realise how skilled the Soviets were in turning the most privileged and respected individuals against the nation that had given them honours and status in the first place. The argument that significant shifts in public consciousness within Western nations could be achieved by specific instructions from Soviet agents conducting a propaganda war against those nations is not nearly so fantastical as it might first appear. Credulity is strained not by imagining that this might have occurred, but by considering it the sole operative factor that applies.

It is also interesting to note that those who would dismiss such arguments in the recent past regarding Soviet interference are the very same people who accept all such arguments today regarding the interference of Putin in Western democracies. It seems self-contradictory to believe that Soviet manipulation achieved no impact on Western public consciousness whilst simultaneously being certain that the KGB-trained Putin can shape Western public consciousness to the extent of distorting US presidential elections or British referendums. In both cases, the rational response is to recognise that such interference took place but that considering it the sole or vital reason for major changes vastly exaggerates the capacity of Soviet or Russian propaganda techniques (whilst simultaneously vastly underestimating the individual agency of the general public and their ability to reach decisions based on their own rational choices).

Bezmonov's description of the reasoning behind Soviet propaganda shifting to a cultural rather than economic battleground is, however, more convincing than any attempt to regard the whole of Cultural Marxism as a movement directed by KGB agents. By the 1980s, any serious analysis would make the failure of communism, as far as economics was concerned, obvious. It was almost impossible for the Soviets to continue to argue that a society in which workers went unpaid, queued for bread and often found there was none available, a society in which the produce was limited and luxuries reserved for senior party officials, was functioning better in terms of access to material comfort than a society in which vast multi-level shopping centres offered a huge variety of goods night and day, and in which far fewer people were threatened with genuine deprivation.

Mutually assured nuclear destruction being as unpalatable to the Soviets as it was to the West further meant that the military competition engaged in with the United States was, ultimately, pointless, even though the Soviets were prepared to damage themselves to some extent in desperately trying to keep up with the spending capacity of the US military industrial complex. But if they could not win the battle economically or militarily, as the late Soviet leaders increasingly recognised, they could still win it culturally. They had no choice but to move to a war of ideas, and in some sense were comfortable in this territory. Marxism, after all, began as an intellectual movement and has always appealed to the classifying and pedagogical instincts of intellectuals.

The description Bezmonov gives of how Soviet propaganda worked is also relevant, because it describes a template of action adopted even by those who have never had any contact with the KGB or even any links to organised socialist or communist movements. Identifying schisms within Western culture, picking away at them, exaggerating the differences, describing all disparities as deliberate and malevolent, identifying some groups as inherent victims and others as inherent oppressors, making all identity confrontational, continually subverting or denigrating all traditional bonds and loyalties within Western society, encouraging a conspiratorial reading of disparities in wealth and status, all of these Soviet techniques perfectly describe Cultural Marxism in action, even amongst those who don't consider themselves Marxists.

12

THE WORTH OF THE WEST

"If they weren't so dangerous and destructive, one could smile and pat the Modern Liberal on the head and tell him how cute he is and go on about the business of being an adult. But he is dangerous and destructive, with the True Believer's very purpose being the total destruction of everything that God and science — most obviously Western Civilization — has ever created... The Modern Liberal will invariably and, in fact, inevitably side with evil over good, wrong over right and the behaviours that lead to failure over those that lead to success."

—Evan Sayet

I WANT PEOPLE TO FIGHT BACK, I WANT PEOPLE to speak out, I want people to denounce the betrayal. For that is what we are witnessing today, and all too many of us simply watch it happening as if it were a drama in which we were not involved. We are living in an age which might well herald the death of Western civilisation, and we greet this tragedy with blithe unconcern. We laugh at those who have the objective intellect and personal integrity required to recognise the perilous situation our society faces, and we concern ourselves with meaningless trivialities or mindless indulgence rather than with preventing the destruction of our entire identity. Self-hate and apathy are the twin swords of the cultural revolutionary, and they cut deep and often. Cultural Marxists rely on us not challenging or recognising what is occurring. They depend upon our silence, and treat it as consent. They require our silence, and will manipulate the law to enforce it, as we have seen with the development of hate speech legislation and the encroachment of successively more draconian responses towards the 'offence' felt by protected groups.

As I write, the European Court of Human Rights has recently declared the existence of a new supposedly universal human right: that of not having your religious sensibilities offended. This laughably fictitious 'right' is not meant to defend Christianity, of course, or Hinduism, or Sikhism, or Buddhism. It is intended solely to appease and accommodate the most fanatical and intolerant religion active today, and it does so by criminalising legitimate criticism. It does not matter whether your criticism is rational or true, only that it offends against Islam. In the 21st century, we see the introduction of a Europe-wide blasphemy law designed to give Islam the same excessive protection from all dissent it enjoys in backwards Islamic nations.

In such a development, we see an institution supposedly founded as a solution to European extremism acting as the guardian and nursemaid of non-European extremism. We see the reversal of several centuries of progress away from purely religious authority, and the denial of the most basic established Western rights of free speech and free thought that are integral parts of what Western identity is. The step that the Ancient Greeks took in criticising the gods and celebrating human reason instead is reversed. The step that Western societies took in limiting the power of the Church is reversed, as sharia law is respected above the individual conscience, and as the right to not be offended somehow comes to supplant the right to speak without fear of assault or imprisonment.

We have reached this point by forgetting the worth of the West. We have forgotten that Western civilisation has given more freedom to more people, more quickly than any other culture. We have forgotten, whilst surrounded by the physical and economic proofs of its efficacy, that Western capitalism is a form of economic liberty. You are free to earn and to prosper. You are free to exchange your labour or inventiveness or skill for adequate remuneration. The free exchange of goods and ideas are aspects of the same respect for the individual. The protection of property rights and the protection of individual rights go hand in hand, for we are each our own first possession. To deny me my property or to seize it by force is the action of a brigand, and unjust or excessive taxation a form of brigandage. My thoughts, too, may be seen as a possession others do not have the right to destroy or to seize or to silence, and are deserving of the same respect as my physical form. Force against either is a perilous thing which governments should be loath to apply, unless I am directly calling for harm to others. I am free to think and speak as I please, and so are others, such that anything I say they may contradict, criticise, question or insult, and vice versa. This is part of who we are, and should not be jettisoned for intolerant arrivals or ignorant barbarians born among us, whether those are immigrant communities, native politicians or self-elected corporate censors.

It was Western civilisation that limited the brute rule of force, that constrained the powers of kings and despots. It was the interplay of power between the Christian Church and the Christian Monarch that gave space for the growth and expression of the rights of the ordinary populace. It was the Roman legacy of law that ultimately denied the efficacy of autocracy, even whilst some Roman emperors served as timeless examples of cruel despotism. It was the inheritance of Greek philosophy and enquiry that taught us to defy established authorities who merely held received opinions, and which gave us the mental tools with which to carve out better political and theological systems. It was the Judeo-Christian heritage that gave us our strongest and most enduring and valuable moral lessons, that defined free will and thereby reminded us of our personal moral responsibility for every action we undertake. We cannot blame our own evils on a deity. We cannot escape our own guilt. We must acknowledge the sin to be forgiven for it. These lessons are the kind of lessons that form decent and responsible individuals and decent and responsible societies.

To summarise the points I have been making thus far:

1. Western civilisation is a shared cultural inheritance covering Europe and the countries most influenced or affected by European colonisation.

2. Western civilisation is, despite the name, not limited by geography. It includes any territory where the same Western cultural heritage dominates. Southern hemisphere nations like Australia or New Zealand, thanks to European colonialism, are included in it today.

3. Western civilisation also largely encompasses the geographic area once termed Christendom. Some regions, notably the Middle East, were once part of Christendom and have been lost to Islam.

4. Western civilisation was born in Ancient Greece. Many of the key identifying features and concepts of Western civilisation derive from the Ancient Greeks. An older historic legacy from the region bordered by the Tigris and Euphrates defined several aspects of civilisation, but is not specifically Western in nature.

5. From the Greeks we inherit philosophy, democracy, aesthetics, art and literature. The Greeks defined the ways we think and feel.

6. The Greek inheritance was taken up and expanded by the Romans. From the Romans we inherit law, language (at least whilst Latin remained the language of the properly educated into the 19th century) and imperialism. The Romans defined the ways we act and rule.

7. The Roman inheritance was taken up and expanded by the Christian Church. From Christianity we inherit our moral law, our respect for human life and dignity, our sense of shared community, and our belief in personal responsibility. Christianity defined the ways in which we rule ourselves and our own baser instincts.

8. Western civilisation has respected the individual more than any other civilisation. It defined and granted human rights more widely than any other culture. It enfranchised more people, both politically and economically, than any other culture.

9. Western civilisation moved from autocracy to democracy. The democratic system of rule is politically integral to Western identity and all contemporary Western nation states are democratic.

10. Western civilisation moved from feudalism to capitalism. The capitalist system of economics is politically integral to Western identity and all contemporary Western nation states are capitalist.

11. Western capitalism, or Western civilisation active in the economic sphere, created the modern global economy. Western capitalism has raised life expectancy and living standards across the globe. The reason that Western economies became dominant globally is because of the inherent advantages of the capitalist system in unleashing economic potential, and not due to exploitation of non-Western societies.

12. Western civilisation gave us Reason and Logic. These are vital tools in reaching an objective understanding of the natural world and a rational understanding of the political world. Deprived of these our understanding of nature does not advance and our politics reverts to barbarism and anarchy.

13. Western civilisation gave us the Socratic Method and the Scientific Method. These are vital tools in turning our objective understanding of the natural world into practical technological solutions, and in turning our rational discussion of ideas into practical philosophies of behaviour. Deprived of these, our technology does not advance and our society reverts to stasis and decline.

14. Western civilisation, via the Scientific Method, has shaped the technological and scientific reality we inhabit today. Western civilisation is responsible for more scientific discoveries and technological inventions than any other human culture.

15. The benefits and advantages of Western civilisation considerably outweigh its negatives and disadvantages. The glories are greater than the crimes, and only those who are historically ignorant or engaged in the Cultural Marxist assault on Western civilisation concentrate solely on the crimes.

16. Western civilisation faces an immediate and growing number of threats. These are existential threats with the potential to end Western civilisation entirely. Such a result would represent an enormous loss for humanity as a whole and cripple hopes of future societal advance.

17. There is both a moral and practical imperative to defend Western civilisation from the threats it faces. Few have recognised this. Eastern European nations recognise it more than Western European nations.

18. Western civilisation is currently led by those who have the least understanding of the perilous situation it faces. In many instances, the political leaders of the West are actively engaged in measures accelerating its decline. This is more of a conspiracy of dunces than a set conspiracy theory, although some of the participants are Cultural Marxists who know exactly what they are doing.

19. The key internal threat is formed by the Cultural Marxist dominance of politics, education and entertainment. People who actively despise Western civilisation are in positions of decision-making authority throughout Western society.

20. The key existential threat is posed by Islam. Islam has been at war with Western civilisation since its formation fourteen centuries ago. Cultural Marxists aid and abet the Islamic assault on Western civilisation and are responsible for importing Islamic populations into the West so that they now form an internal as well as an external threat.

Book Two

The Heritage of
Cultural Marxism

"History has been stolen from us and
replaced with guilt-inducing lies."

—Stefan Molyneux

It is a central contention of this book that
the term Cultural Marxism covers a variety of anti-Western ideologies,
memes, organisations and groups together with the behaviours and agendas
they follow. One of the great weaknesses in the arguments of those defending Western civilisation is that they can easily fall into the trap of imagining that there is some singular cause or force behind Cultural Marxism.
There is not. These are an alliance of groups united only in their trained
and engrained hatred of Western civilisation. They are, if you like, a hydra
with no controlling intelligence.

The genuine far right, who by any rational interpretation are a tiny
movement far smaller amongst Western patriots and nationalists than, say,
Islamists are within Islamic culture, will fall back on the oldest conspiracy
theory there is and note the Jewish dominance amongst groups like the

Frankfurt School, or among prominent Cultural Marxists today. Soros is again an example of this error, with some using his Jewish ethnic background as some sort of explanation of his leftist cultural interventions. The vileness of anti-Semitism is very much on the rise again, but primarily driven today by the Left rather than the Right. Suffice it to say that the idea that Cultural Marxism is a Jewish conspiracy is one which, in its falsehood and idiocy, I will not spare much time bothering to consider. No such explanation ever considers exactly what the Jewish people would gain by the destruction of the West or why they would simultaneously construct a nation state in Israel that upholds the core values of Western civilisation and suffers daily as a result of the assaults of the same barbaric Islamism that threatens the rest of the Western world. The very fact that leftists so irrationally despise the only Jewish state on the planet should tell right-wing thinkers that the Jews are not their oppressors in any way whatsoever. In thinking they are, the far right mirror the conspiratorial thinking patterns of the hard Left and even point the finger of blame in the same direction.

What is true, however, is that no political movement, no ideology and no great shift in public consciousness occurs without moments of foreshadowing, without deep roots in precursor movements and cultural developments over centuries. The tapestry of history and society is such that the tracing of influence can never really end, so it is incumbent upon us to sift through earlier examples of similar or formative thinking and focus on the most significant ones which have had the greatest impact.

We have already discussed to some extent the deliberate Soviet influence on the rapid spread of Cultural Marxist attitudes, so now we should also consider those earlier moments of cultural crisis within Western civilisation that Cultural Marxism so frequently refers back to, draws selective lessons from, and displays similar characteristics to. As well as Communism, these are Puritanism, prior Revolutions (French, American and Russian), Anarchism, Anti-Colonialism, Feminism and the 1960s Counter-Cultural

Revolution and academic Postmodernism. I will by no means attempt any exhaustive analysis of these very significant cultural movements, only trace some of the elements they share with Cultural Marxism and how these historical moments have been deliberately reconfigured and misinterpreted in ways that support the Cultural Marxists and lend them an intellectual legitimacy their shallow readings of history would not otherwise possess.

13

PURITANISM

*"No son of mine should ever take the side of
the Puritans: that is always an error."*

—Oscar Wilde, *A Woman of No Importance*

AT FIRST SIGHT, IT MIGHT SEEM THAT PURITANISM
could not possibly have anything in common with Cultural Marxism.
Puritanism was, of course, a Christian religious movement, and many Cultural
Marxists are self-professed atheists with a particular distaste for Christianity.
In this sense, Puritanism and Cultural Marxism represent opposite ends of
a theological spectrum. A base assumption of the Cultural Marxist is that
Christianity is to be mocked and traduced, that Christianity supported and
supports unjust Western value judgements and that Christianity's claims of
benevolence are contradicted by atrocities and sins committed by Christians
(often in the name of their faith) throughout history.

The Cultural Marxist assumes generally that all religions are supersti-
tious and false, but specifically that Christianity is especially hypocritical,
dishonest and worthless. Since Christianity is the traditional faith of the
ultimate oppressor group, namely white people of European descent, and
since Christianity is tied to Western identity and history, it naturally follows
that Christianity is especially deserving of censure. It is, in classic Marxist

terms, an "opium of the masses" which must be resisted. And yet if we look at methodology and attitude towards any part of Western civilisation that does not share their intentions, some telling similarities between Puritanism and Cultural Marxism rapidly emerge. The reality is that the differences between Puritanism and Cultural Marxism are more superficial in nature than the similarities between both movements.

The Puritans were a radical and political branch of Christianity. Unlike Protestantism as a whole, they did not simply demand a return to the simplicities of teaching derived directly from biblical sources, nor did they merely seek the curtailment of specific ecclesiastical corruptions. Martin Luther listed particular offences which sparked the Protestant rejection of the Catholic Church, but the Puritans did not limit their objections to Rome or to Catholicism. They rejected even moderate versions of Protestantism and framed their weltanschaung around the notion that the whole of non-Puritan society represented sinful wickedness.

The Puritans in particular rejected the practical religious compromises that had evolved in England from the Elizabethan settlement onwards. Elizabeth I's quintessentially English compromise that she would not make windows into men's souls could never accommodate Puritan fanaticism, nor could the Manichean and reductive Puritan division of society between the pure and the impure cope with the irritant of monarchs who were once Catholic or who were suspected of retaining Catholic sympathies. Puritanism represented one of the most profound moments in which a segment of Western civilisation fully rejected the remainder of Western civilisation, and as such bears strong parallels with the thinking of Cultural Marxists today.

However much individual contemporary Cultural Marxists self-identify as atheists, their entire ideology is suffused with religious thinking. Cultural Marxism is a moral system based on a reading of good and evil in perpetual conflict. The tools by which Western man escapes theological fetters on thought and speech have been, after all, specifically traduced by Cultural

Marxism. The reason and logic that would limit the theological instinct are dismissed by Cultural Marxist theory as Western prejudices which exist solely to justify an unequal and oppressive distribution of resources. This means that as well as crippling the capacity of the society they inhabit for making clear-headed, objective choices based on sound principles of logic, the Cultural Marxists deny to themselves these same key tools of Western thought.

Just as the Puritan tended towards a self-denying asceticism in terms of physical sustenance and pleasure, so too does the Cultural Marxist tend towards an ideological asceticism which is deeply suspicious of the enjoyment to be derived from clear, unbiased thought. Ideas are policed with the same rigour under Cultural Marxism as they are under Puritanism. Those breaking the codes of thought imposed by Cultural Marxism are, like those breaking the taboos enforced by Puritan morality, guilty of sins which must be punished.

The moral vanity of Cultural Marxists is one of their defining characteristics. The ideology they follow defines the entirety of good and evil and therefore offers them the comfort of being and feeling good regardless of their individual behaviours. This is why a Cultural Marxist would, for example, consider alleged sexual predators and even people they know to be sexual predators to be good people, even whilst being ready to demonise and persecute political rivals on the basis of unproven allegations of sexual misconduct. Harvey Weinstein and Bill Clinton were good people because they were contemporary liberals fully signed up to the Cultural Marxist agenda. They spoke about female rights and empowerment and they paid lip service to notions such as the glass ceiling or the idea that Western society enforces a patriarchy. This meant that they were good, even whilst any traditional moral view would have noted not their political affiliations as being of primary importance, but their personal actions.

Similarly, in the Women's March against Trump, one of the primary organisers was a woman who had served time for kidnapping a man and torturing him to death. But this woman was a prominent feminist. The fact that she had inserted a metal rod into a man's anus against his will and ended this and other depravities by killing him registered as less serious an issue, to her and others, than Trump's use of the word "pussy" in a private conversation when boasting about sexual conquests being easier for men who happen to be billionaires. The contemporary ideology, the Cultural Marxist hierarchy of victimhood, defines any feminist — even a proven killer — as a victim, not as an oppressor. At the same time, it defines any man as already guilty, by dint of being a man or, even worse, a Republican. No real proof was needed, for example, before Kavanaugh was considered guilty. The presumption of innocence before guilt is proven in a court of law is, after all, another of those despicable inventions of Western civilisation, formulated by inherently vile white males.

Where you sit on the political spectrum and the language you use — whether it is politically correct or not — matters more to the Cultural Marxist than any action you perform. Verbal crudities from nationalists or traditionalists are real offences, whereas serious sexual assaults or proven acts of violence, or incitement towards them, if committed by fellow Cultural Marxists, do not register as crimes at all. Similarly, the Cultural Marxist intention matters far more than any practical consequence of a political action. Merkel's call to migrants welcoming them to Germany is a good act because it is a Cultural Marxist act, and any resulting rise in crime or loathsome molestation that results for the women of Germany from such a policy is immaterial. Indeed, as far as I am aware, no mainstream liberal politician in the whole of the Western world, having supported open borders policies, has ever bothered to meet the families of affected victims of rape or murder by illegal immigrants or migrants they have welcomed. Trump, of course, the bestial Neanderthal who spreads hate and division, has bothered to visit such families and listen to their grim narratives.

The Cultural Marxist assumption of moral superiority despite repeated evidence to the contrary is a consequence of a religious thinking centred on loyalty to its ideology, a type of religious thinking shared by the Puritans of the past and the Islamists of the present. Since non-Cultural-Marxists are inherently evil, any evil done towards them is justified and in fact good. We see this thinking at work in groups like Antifa, where their own use of political violence is excused by the pre-emptive demonisation of any group they are violent towards. The 'its ok to punch a Nazi' self-justification allows Antifa or Momentum in the UK to deny freedom of speech and thought (real classical liberal values) and engage in political violence against otherwise peaceful groups and demonstrations by ludicrously assuming that anyone they are violent towards is a Nazi.

Mainstream conservatives, classical liberals, free speech advocates, opponents of the genuinely fascistic tendencies within Islam, otherwise apolitical patriots or opponents of mass immigration, even entire classes like the white working class, are targeted and considered 'Nazis' because this justifies the thing that is the real underlying addiction of the hard Left: unrestrained power and its violent expression. This drive towards violence is fuelled by the Cultural Marxist's hatred of the rational tools of Western thought. In the absence of persuasion other than via appeals to emotion and ideology, violence fills the gap when such persuasion (or propaganda) fails. And in the religious self-identification of themselves as enlightened or perfected human beings, following the 'true' and 'progressive' ideology which is destined to lead humanity towards a better future, Cultural Marxists become incapable of recognising the gulf between their claims of purity and the morally impure and violent methodologies they consistently deploy. They cannot see that they behave like Nazis more frequently than those they target because they are convinced of their inherent goodness, which is derived merely by subscribing to Cultural Marxist attitudes.

This moral self-blindness, shared with fanatical religious groups such as the Puritans of the past or the Islamists of the present, is not even limited solely to those Cultural Marxists who actively participate in violence, but is active throughout all branches of Cultural Marxism. An example of this can be found in the mainstream media's responses to internal political violence driven by Cultural Marxist groups within the US. The anti-Trump Women's March movement as described above has included a convicted murderer among its key organisers, as well as other individuals who have unsavoury records of anti-semitism or misandry.

Mainstream Democrat political figures like Nancy Pelosi have flirted with the language of actual insurrection by calling for 'government uprisings' against the democratically elected President. Congresswoman Maxine Waters called for physical confrontation and harassment of all members of the Trump administration. Alexandra Ocasio-Cortez called for protestors to invade, occupy and control ICE facilities and airports. Democrat Congressman Tom Souzzi implied that people should take up arms against Trump, saying that those opposed to his Presidency should refer to their 2nd Amendment right to bear arms. New York Governor Andrew Cuomo stated that Trump-supporting Republicans were 'extreme' and 'had no place in New York'. House Democrat Steve Cohen wondered "where are our military folks?" as he called for the US military to overthrow Trump in July 2018 on Twitter.

Anti-Trumpism is perhaps the branch of Cultural Marxism which has been most obviously barbaric and theological. Trump is quite clearly a Satan figure, and the solutions proposed to deal with Trump are more often than not violent. There is a hard puritanical element of pure hatred running through 'liberal' commentaries and responses to Trump and Trump voters. The beheading of Trump, mirroring Islamist fascination with this method of execution as well as the guillotines of the French Revolution, was a popular trope amongst the harder core sections of the self-styled 'Resistance' to

Trump, even before comedienne Kathy Griffin played out her own political beheading fantasy to the detriment of her commercial viability. Whilst Griffin faced a backlash for that, other prominent Anti-Trumpers have been just as violent and puritanical in their declarations, with no response from the mainstream media. And no response, remember, in a culture that polices thought and speech more thoroughly than democracies ever have before, and that tells us that 'hate speech' is an actual crime. Depending, of course, on who it is directed at.

In the wake of the Charlottesville clashes between violent extremists of both the Right and the Left, Trump's entirely rational assertion that there were violent individuals and groups on both sides, together with his condemnation of all political violence, caused fury amongst the Cultural Marxists of mainstream media and entertainment precisely because it refused to limit criticism solely to the Right. How extreme, one might ask, are the views of those who are infuriated by a condemnation of all violence and who see that as support for white supremacy?

We have, of course, witnessed a growing tendency towards direct physical attacks or aggressive harassment from Cultural Marxists towards those who refuse to share their prejudices and particularly towards anyone who defends traditional right-wing or conservative values in a public manner. Pro-Brexit figures like Nigel Farage or Jacob Rees-Mogg have been the victims of these intimidatory tactics. Farage has received death threats and is regularly greeted with harassment in public, such as when daring to risk a Sunday family lunch, which was disrupted despite the presence of his children. Rees-Mogg similarly found his six-year-old child addressed by an angry Cultural Marxist bereft of even the most rudimentary of moral codes when it comes to behaviour towards children. Prominent figures of the Right can, by their mere presence and existence, stir Cultural Marxist activists (particularly in academia) to violence, as testified by riots attending or preventing speeches by the likes of Milo Yiannopoulos or Sargon of Akkad (the latter not even being right-wing but frequently identified as such by those entirely ignorant of the actual content he delivers).

The policing of speech and thought occupies a primary place in Cultural Marxist activity, just as it does in all totalitarian belief systems and with the same sinister and proscriptive intent it possessed for the Puritans of the sixteenth and seventeenth centuries. Political correctness is the (on the surface secular) modern form of Puritan policing of language, driven by the same sense of religious exceptionalism. Like the Puritan, the Cultural Marxist knows that they have the right to dictate our words and deeds because they are good, because they are purifying both discourse and society, purging it of unclean elements of dissension. Like the Puritan, the Cultural Marxist believes that their ideology alone should inform and shape politics and social life, and that any deviation from that ideology represents wickedness. Like the Puritan, the Cultural Marxist has a simplistic, reductive worldview that is not moderated by rationality or circumstance, but which gives absolute instruction regarding the good and evil of every action and every individual.

Like the Puritan, the Cultural Marxist is working towards a societal vision, the construction of a City of God (or a borderless World) ruled entirely by the same ideological stance. It is assumed that the political control of society by the ideology will in some mysterious way lead to the perfection of the human species itself, a future Rapture in which the inevitable triumph of the ideology will be made manifest to all. Until then, it is likewise assumed that a strict division exists between the righteous, who work towards this epiphany, and everyone else, who hinders it. Like the Puritan, the Cultural Marxist sees control of education as a vital component of the process by which the ideology shapes and moulds society towards the desired totality of control (Puritans were as keen on literacy as Cultural Marxists are on academic conformity).

We see the same Puritan connection in many Remain and elite responses to the modern heresy that is Brexit. The EU is treated increasingly as a religious sacred object rather than as a failing and generally quite corrupt institution of dubious benefit. The break from the Treaty of Rome has been treated in the same way as the Protestant Reformation and break from the papal authority of Rome was treated by the most ardent Catholics — as a heretical act that must be reversed. Brexiteers are recast as evil sinners and wrongdoers, either thoughtless dupes if mere voters or, if prominent enough, Machiavellian schemers with purely malign purposes.

Project Fear, the sustained campaign of negative propaganda regarding Brexit which has been in continuous operation since 2016, is perhaps the most Puritan propaganda campaign we have seen in the United Kingdom since the 17th century. Economic doom is prophesised with all the lack of logical coherence and depth of passion to be found in much earlier sermons of hellfire and damnation. Almost any proposed negative impact of Brexit, no matter how trivial (difficulty obtaining sandwiches), unlikely (increase of sexually transmitted diseases) or apocalyptic (planes dropping from the skies) is considered as a serious rather than hysterical point. The post-Brexit future becomes a playground for the religious imagination of the true believers in the European Project, with wars, pestilence and ruin following like the four horsemen of the apocalypse. This is connected to Cultural Marxism in that the EU is aligned with and consequent upon key Cultural Marxist attitudes towards Western nation states (it is the political vehicle for the delivery of the destruction of traditional European nation states, the marshalling of European resentment towards the United States, and the gradual creation of the borderless future the Cultural Marxist desires).

Remain arguments in favour of the EU, whilst far less frequently expressed than the hellfire prophecies of damnation which constitute the anti-Brexit narrative, are also largely of a religious nature. The European Project is again a totalitarian and utopian vision, a City of God. The EU is supposed to have protected Europeans from war. It is the hope of peace, the promise of fellowship, the bond of progress and harmony. All of these are theological rather than practical ideas. A pragmatist can quite swiftly point to the unemployment rates of Southern Europe to dispute the utopian promises made and believed regarding EU economics. But even in the economic sphere, the idea of the EU as provider is more powerful for many (including most of those in Western governments) than the reality of the EU as vicious creditor for nations like Greece, or money-hungry, demanding supplicant for nations like the UK.

Similarly, the most fanatical zealots of the European Project are all committed Cultural Marxists identifying every evil of history with European nation states. Nationalism is to these New Puritans what Catholicism was to the old ones. In the headquarters of the EU is a plaque making this explicit, firmly blaming the existence of nation states for all the horrors of World War One and World War Two. That almost all of those who defeated Nazism were nationalists, as were even most of the conscientious objectors of WWI, does not register at all. Nations are evil not by what they do but by what they are. Supranational bodies are moral not by what they do but by what they are. The moral excuses and pre-set roles of victim and oppressor that Cultural Marxism applies on an individual level are also applied on a geopolitical level. Both Merkel and Macron have delivered speeches against nationalism that are essentially expressions of Puritan faith. The nations of the world are viewed as Jesus viewed them from the desert heights when offered them by Satan.

Like Antifa, the EU itself is also a self-consciously antifascist organisation with a lamentable tendency towards fascist methodologies (witness Macron's militaristic response to the Yellow Vests, witness the EU's persistent contempt for democracy, witness the Spanish government's thuggish response, endorsed by the EU, to the Catalan referendum). Again and again, we see pious declarations of what the EU creates, intends or upholds, contrasted with the grim reality of how the EU destroys, acts and demeans. This contrast makes faith in the EU a religious article of belief just like Puritanism, a psychological choice to concentrate on what the ideology promises rather than on what it actually delivers.

The similarities between Cultural Marxism and Puritanism are therefore the similarities of a shared psychology founded on absolute moral self-regard and self-blindness. The question of 'who watches the watchmen?' simply cannot occur to those possessed of this psychological profile. There is also such a shared seriousness and all-encompassing religious belief in the rectitude of the social projects and changes undertaken in the name of the ideology that both the Puritan and the Cultural Marxist lose the ability to recognise exaggeration or distortion. They do not inhabit a nuanced world of particular moments analysed objectively. They inhabit a moving drama of religious battle with sinners and the sinful world that sinners create.

This means, of course, that they cannot realise when their own ideological choices become ridiculous in the eyes of more rational observers. Fighting imaginary Nazis is as serious a business as fighting real ones. Just like a Puritan, a Cultural Marxist can easily be drawn into positions which are almost a spoof of their creed and, indeed, recognising a well-written spoof amongst many of the more absurd declarations of Cultural Marxism becomes increasingly difficult. Puritans could ban Christmas and think that a reasonable, non-ridiculous act, just as Cultural Marxists can laughably insist on renaming the same celebration so as not to upset minorities.

We see this un-self-aware seriousness at its greatest in academia. Academic Cultural Marxists are even less capable of nuanced self-reflection than their fellows in the media, entertainment or government. Cultural Marxist academic journals have accepted and published spoof articles designed solely to illustrate the proliferation of meaningless jargon and evidence-free nonsense in such fields as gender studies. It is their very seriousness which leaves them vulnerable to such mockery. There is in all of this a strong element of religious delusion. The Cultural Marxist is, like Young Goodman Brown in Hawthorne's reflection on his own Puritan ancestors, engaged in uncovering witches and heresy, whether they are real or merely figments of the searcher's own imagination.

Sometimes this is the single most telling similarity between Cultural Marxism and Puritanism. They are united by their humourlessness. Saving the world is a serious business, after all, especially when you are trying to save it from imaginary problems. Anyone who has sat through the broadcast of a BBC Radio Four topical news quiz or the routines of a feminist standup, or watched political sitcoms like C4's wretchedly hypocritical hatefest 'Home' is well aware that Cultural Marxists understand comedy in the same way that peadophiles understand consent. It's certainly a topic they are interested in, but it's unwise to trust their conclusions about what it is. For most of them, comedy is one long, satisfying, masturbatory Sneer, which if publicly performed represents an orgy of self-regard in which a liberal audience laughs, not so much because anything is funny, but because the mutual stroking of a few well-worn ideas is pleasurable to them. Cultural Marxists are only ever funny by accident, when their absurdity is self-evident, and always fanatically serious when trying to be funny. They are Puritans in power, using a bastardised form of satire to defend rather than critique the Establishment. They aim their humour at the powerless rather than the powerful, at the Brexiteer rather than the bureaucrat, at the Trump voter rather than the Democrat donor, at the poorest rather than the richest.

14

THE AMERICAN REVOLUTION

*"The spirit of resistance to government is so valuable on
certain occasions that I wish it to always be kept alive."*

—Thomas Jefferson

THE AMERICAN REVOLUTION, OR WAR OF

Independence, between 1775 and 1783 marked the first significant reverse
of the British imperial project (although it should also be remembered that
the most expansive phase of European colonialism, for Britain and other
major European powers, occurred after this, with the scramble for Africa
and the humiliations suffered by China and others in the 19th century). It
established not only the political right of revolution, which of course had
been manifested earlier, but was a template by which such revolution could
actually achieve its aims. The deployment of voluntary militias, the concept
of an army of citizens selecting themselves for military action rather than an
army of professionals imposed on citizens by the State, is not only central
to the self-mythology of the US (and enshrined in the 2nd Amendment,
which complicates the line between national law and individual liberty even
today) but a precursor of the anti-colonial movements of the 20th century
which would unravel European global hegemony subsequent to WWII. The
Americans themselves would, of course, suffer their greatest humiliation

in Vietnam based on guerrilla tactics directly descended from their own rejection of British power.

The relationship of the War of Independence to contemporary Cultural Marxism is both instructive and complicated. On the one hand, it might be thought that this rejection of British imperialism would be seen in a positive light by Cultural Marxists today who often use that imperialism as a short-hand for all political systems they despise. They act as if that imperialism were some active force it is necessary to fight and protest against today (irre-spective of the complete absence of any imperial intent from Britain since the Suez Crisis). In a typical display of both linguistic and moral legerdermain, however, contemporary Cultural Marxists have no feeling of affinity or sense of respect towards the American achievement of independence. In their eyes, this was simply one group of middle-aged white males supplanting another. Hatred of the US and its history is as heavily woven into the fabric of Cultural Marxism as similar hatreds of Britain and Israel are.

Of course, the surface reason for the Cultural Marxist refusal to see the War of Independence and the foundation of the United States as a signifi-cant precursor movement or as something to be viewed in a positive light derives from the US assumption of superpower status in the wake of British decline. Whilst it is certainly true to say that from the outset, the United States has made foreign policy blunders and bears some blame for negative global reactions to US power, such blunders are to an extent an inevitable consequence of significant military and economic reach. Every extremely powerful nation has greater opportunity to do both good and evil on a greater scale than less significant rivals.

This consequence of success has been true of the Spanish, the French, the British, the Russians and the Americans in the last five hundred years, and is likely to be true of the Chinese and Indians in the future. But Cultural Marxism refuses to acknowledge any of the positive contributions of US power or of US society, and is tellingly unmoved even by the idealistic pronouncements of the US Constitution, its Enlightenment founders, and of every American administration in history. They give no credit to Woodrow Wilson's support of anti-imperialism, for instance, or the increasing use of US power to speed the process of enfranchisement and independence for all those nations and peoples who had existed under colonial rule.

As ever in politics, the idealistic pronouncements can easily be compared to a grubbier reality. Jefferson could declare in the magnificent cadences of complete assurance that make the Declaration of Independence such a powerful document that all men are created equal and that the truth of this is self-evident, whilst simultaneously being a slave owner who quite casually denied, in the morality of his time, "life, liberty and the pursuit of happiness" to human beings he himself owned as chattels, including those he had sired (primarily thought to have occurred via Martha Hemmings, his slave who also happened to be his deceased wife Martha's half-sister). Cultural Marxists are as swift to point out these contradictions of the past as they are slow to recognise them in their present stances.

The truth, however, is that the Jeffersonian contrast of public idealism and private selfishness is of course not so stark as it appears today, since more men than merely Jefferson could accommodate the cognitive dissonance of simultaneously perceiving oneself as a defender of human liberty and a supporter of slavery (on the basis that a 'benevolent' enslavement of a black slave was little different from the authority a parent wielded over a child, and required the same responsibilities of good care. A view of slavery, of course, consistent with that expressed in the Koran, in case anyone is tempted to see this as an instance of uniquely Western hypocrisy).

Our horror of such a position is both real and just, and represents the cultural moral advancement that Western civilisation has championed, but it is equally true that applying that horror retroactively to past lives without any nuance is to tramp through history like some pious censor rather than an objective recorder of events. The Cultural Marxist, of course, does exactly this, in relation to Jefferson, US history and all Western history generally (whilst applying none of this moral loathing to fourteen centuries of Islamic links with slavery and oppression, or to Chinese, Japanese or African involvement in similar crimes).

The great irony here is that it is in this moral and racial selectivity that the contemporary Cultural Marxist is most like the founding fathers of the United States. Just as Jefferson loved all liberty with some racial exclusions, Cultural Marxists claim to detest all oppression with some racial exclusions. Just as the writers of the US Constitution could see the letter of their words on liberty as being more significant than the tenor of their actions, so too does the contemporary Cultural Marxist excuse himself and his allies from the moral judgements they impose on others. Like Jefferson, the declarative trumps the active, which is precisely what makes it so easy for Cultural Marxists to excuse their own vices.

15

The French Revolution

"Their resistance was made to concession; their revolt was from protection; their blow was aimed at a hand holding out graces, favours and immunities."

—Edmund Burke

During the September massacres of the French Revolution in 1792, the Princesse de Lambelle, a close friend and confidante of Marie Antoinette, was dragged from the cell she had been imprisoned in at La Force Prison and brutally murdered by a howling mob, who then mutilated her body and decapitated her. The severed head was fixed on a pike and paraded in front of the window of the room where Marie Antoinette was held captive, whilst members of the barbaric and exultant mob mockingly called for the former Queen to 'kiss the lips of her intimate'. This grotesque incident was only one of hundreds of murders to take place in the name of the Revolution in 1792, and was followed in 1793 by even further bloodshed during the ten-month period of the Reign of Terror, during which the Jacobin faction seized control of the National Convention and gave Robespierre's Committee of Public Safety free rein to murder at least another 17,000 citizens.

Just as the British philosopher and politician Edmund Burke had warned presciently in 1790 in his book *Reflections on the Revolution in France*, written before the Terror, at a point at which many were welcoming the Revolution as a moral good, the utopian promises of the 'empire of light and reason' had descended into the most brutal forms of barbarism and oppression, far in excess of the sins of the Ancien Régime it replaced. Indeed, at the symbolic moment that the Bastille fell, still celebrated in France today as the moment of rejection of ancient tyranny in favour of modern enlightenment, the notorious prison was largely empty. Whilst the economic incompetence and social inequality of France's feudal system and its last rulers was obvious, these were not the products of deliberate malice, nor were the propaganda pieces of inflammatory hate circulated prior to the Revolution, in which the royal family and their court were depicted as incestuous, sex-crazed maniacs presiding over bacchanalian orgies whilst the people suffered, remotely realistic.

Those unsure of the relevance of all this to the topic of Cultural Marxism fail to acknowledge the enormous influence the French Revolution has held in the minds of political radicals and reformers not only in the 18th century itself but ever since. Subsequent revolutions, particularly the Russian Revolution of 1917 and Communist uprisings globally since then, have followed the French Revolution almost as if it were a template of action, a process to be repeated again and again until some different ultimate outcome results. Utopian declarations are followed by brutal actions. Proclamations of liberty give way to mass imprisonments, and then to systemic and widespread political murders. Incompetent rulers described as tyrants give way to self-elected reformers who are far more tyrannical than those they supplant.

Revolutionaries ever since the French Revolution have been both inspired by its success and blind to its failings, and indeed can in many cases be defined as revolutionaries by the extent to which they fail to recognise the human cost of the French Revolution or fail to care about the victims of their own endeavours. The French Revolution helped shape the European political consciousness for centuries, most obviously in France itself but throughout every nation touched by the Revolutionary armies or those that followed under Napoleon's imperial command. These influences include both the psychological and the practical, such as the legacy of Napoleonic law codes which remain a fundamental distinction between Continental law and its methodologies and British law.

In many ways, the French Revolution can be seen as the first fully modern uprising, a rebellion which did not seek to remove particular hated advisors or policies but which aimed for a fundamental, radical and complete change of a political system. Whilst the propaganda attending it was highly personal, scurrilous and charged with individual hatreds and animosities, the royal family were never the sole target and were hated as much as symbols of the entire order as they were as individual human beings. Marie Antoinette in particular suffered more from this symbolic status, with a vast gulf opening between her largely trivial personal excesses and the symbolic import of her status as a hated and foreign Queen representative of every excess of any person loyal to the monarchist cause.

Earlier European revolutions did not have this character or descend so swiftly into outright barbarism. The earlier back one goes in the history of revolution, the more a distinction grows between a rebellion which is perceived to be serving a restorative function and an uprising which has an entirely destructive intent. Something like the Pilgrimage of Grace in King Henry VIII's reign, for example, was about the reclamation of a tradition, not the destruction of all tradition. Earlier feudal rebellions assumed either that the monarch was worthy but poorly advised, and therefore demanded the removal of key councillors rather than of the monarch himself, or that the tainted monarch who had proven himself unworthy could be replaced by a suitably qualified alternative. The English Civil War was especially bloody amongst pre-French Revolution internal conflicts because of the elements of it that were purely destructive towards established social order, whilst the Glorious Revolution of 1688 was bloodless because of its restorative intent and because the salutary lessons of the Civil War were still uppermost in all minds.

The difference between restorative and destructive rebellion is thus the difference between replacing a chess piece and smashing the board to pieces. The first accepts the rules and conditions of the game as natural and just no matter the current situation; that is, that it is natural for a nation state to be ruled by a monarch and for that monarch to come from certain select families, or that it is natural for a Christian religion to guide and influence the politics of the nation whether or not that religion is Protestant or Catholic. The second kind of rebellion represents a rejection of all the accepted rules and political assumptions that have moderated social behaviour up to that point.

A key schism that opened in Western European civilisation that hinges on the French Revolution and has been little mentioned by mainstream political commentators is that between restorative rebellion and destructive rebellion. Restorative rebellion is part of the natural evolution of a society and does not need to descend into barbarism (it can do but will not do so automatically). This is because it refers back to an established moral order that both sides, no matter how violently opposed, still accept. A monarch faced with such rebellion is aware of its limited nature, and if successful in defeating it, only has to respond in a limited manner. The leaders are executed, not their entire families, for example, or rebellious individuals are suppressed, not entire groups or factions to which they belong (some peasants might be killed, but not all kulaks). The fundamental principles on which the power of the ruler depends have not been undermined, so to retain that power does not require the complete removal of the class that posed a limited threat to it.

Similarly, if a restorative rebellion is successful, the actions taken will be limited solely to those that serve the restorative function (a Catholic is placed on the throne, or a specific advisor is removed, or a set policy is changed). Part of the skill of handling an uprising can be seen in the capacity of the ruler or ruling class to keep that uprising particular and specific, to make it a restorative rather than destructive rebellion. This applies to post-monarchical as well as monarchical systems of rule. A government can survive a poll tax revolt where it would not survive a revolt about it being the government (the poll tax riots and protests of 1990 which involved millions of participants in the UK were solved in traditional restorative fashion. The hated policy was dropped, Prime Minister Thatcher was duly removed and replaced, and the Conservatives, having restored the pre-riot equilibrium, managed to win a subsequent election and govern for another seven years).

The distinction between restorative and destructive rebellion is also defined by national differences within the histories of specific Western states, most noticeably Britain and France. France has had several destructive rebellions, rebellions which required a complete change of political system, beginning with the French Revolution and subsequently inspired by it. So has Russia, beginning with the Russian Revolution (though arguably the reforms of Peter the Great or of a few other Tsarist monarchs could be said to be as seismic and to have required the same level of brutality). Most Continental European nations retained absolutist monarchies long past the point where the British had developed a constitutional monarchy, whilst the French Revolution's first draft of a constitutional monarchy proved stillborn. This meant that when revolution came, it had to be more complete.

Whilst the British certainly have an experience of internal conflict as brutal as most modern revolutions in the form of the English Civil War, the British political system learned from that experience in ways that continental Europe did not learn from, say, the French Wars of Religion or the Thirty

Years' War that brought horrific destruction to regions in central Europe. Subsequent British politics was unusually stable for a good reason.

The British have had, throughout their history, a natural tendency towards the restorative solution and the political compromise that allows societies to evolve through conflict rather than remain permanently mired within it. This is perhaps the key to understanding why Britain, composed of small but sometimes violently opposed constituent nations, rose to world dominance in the nineteenth century and seemed to learn best the lessons of Greek democracy and Roman cunning (a national facility that sadly seems much faded in recent times). For Eastern Europe, the experience of Soviet rule again resulted in sustained tyranny and again required more complete revolution, ensuring that their experience of democracy is very different from that of Western European nations, even whilst they remain part of Western civilisation as a whole.

Burke understood the difference between the British model of restorative rebellion and what was occurring in France as he wrote in 1790, which is why he could accurately predict the horrors to come. He knew the difference between a Peasant's Revolt (against specific injustices, framed as an appeal to existing authority) and the chaos of pure revolution or, worse, the directed malice of those determined to exploit such a moment for a radical and permanent shift in political system. Looking through British history, one can see a long unbroken thread of restorative rebellion, all harking back essentially to the idea of the rights of freeborn Englishmen, which existed even before the creation of the nation state that would bear their racial name. The Magna Carta in 1215 references these pre-Norman rights.

Every appeal to every English monarch for justice was based on a sometimes half-conscious memory of Anglo-Saxon kingship and the limited nature of that kingship, which had always included a recognition of the necessity of consent from the governed towards those who govern. The often brutal early Normans had no conception of such a thing in their version of what it meant to rule, but unlike their continental cousins, such a lack of awareness was, piece by piece and century by century, instilled in them by the stubborn belief, which never left the English mind, that every man had freedoms that even kings could not trespass at will. And what kings cannot do, neither can Church, nor President, nor Prime Minister, nor Parliament. The Glorious Revolution of 1688 and the Bill of Rights gave a firm statement of this understanding, as well as providing a perfect illustration in its bloodless contrast with the French Revolution of the difference between restorative and destructive rebellions.

The difference between restorative rebellion and destructive rebellion, then, is a difference not only of degree but also of morality, not only between the evolution of a political system towards greater freedom and the replacement of a political system with greater tyranny, but also the difference between the Western civilisation of Europe and the Western civilisation of the Anglosphere (of Britain, the United States, Canada, Australia and New Zealand). Even at the start of the American Revolution, George Washington was referencing the British tradition of restorative rebellion by stating that he sought only the confirmation of his rights as a freeborn Englishman. This is why the War of Independence could fashion something new that nevertheless worked and took its place in the history of Western nations advancing democracy and freedom.

By contrast, those who follow the model of the French Revolution replace incompetence with tyranny and, whilst clothed in utopian language about liberty, equality and fraternity, instead welcome state brutality, absolutism and hatred. Any revolution that requires the complete destruction of all the traditional institutions of a nation and the concentration of all power in revolutionary hands will, as Burke knew, inevitably witness the fallible human beings who have seized such authority misuse it, precisely because nothing remains to prevent them from doing so. This has been the trajectory of every Communist revolution through history and it is the trajectory that

Cultural Marxism will also follow unless it is stopped before its seizure of power is complete.

How long will it be, for example, before the cry of "equality" claims as many modern victims as the old cry of "egalité"? Victims not only of legalised injustices, not only of being denied genuine equality of opportunities in the forced pursuit of equality of outcome, but of actual violence and bloodshed? In some senses, such victims already exist. Whilst Cultural Marxist calls for uprisings against Trump or Brexit have not resulted in actual revolutions, there are already those who have directly suffered, unnecessarily, in Western nations owing to Cultural Marxist policies. The children in Britain raped by migrant communities, by mainly Pakistani men of Muslim faith, are the victims of Cultural Marxism as well as of Islam. The women abused in Sweden or Germany are such victims, as well as the bullied and beaten children that are attacked by migrants throughout Europe.

Even amongst the migrants themselves, we should recognise that the vast numbers abused or killed in journeys to the West are the victims of the Cultural Marxist policies and politicians (like Merkel) who encouraged those dangerous journeys. The insane combination of a domestic policy that encourages mass migration and a foreign policy that engages in fruitless wars with widespread bombing, the two most obvious policy effects of Cultural Marxist thinking, will continue to claim victims both at home and abroad, even without revolutionary uprisings in Western nations themselves, though both policies make such uprisings more likely.

The French Revolution and Cultural Marxism share some essential hypocrisies. Both are products of the Enlightenment and of a penchant for systemisation and analysis that can be seen as a twisted perversion of the Western tradition of intellectual enquiry. The Enlightenment leaders of the French Revolution were drawn from the emergent middle class of profes-sionals, writers, lawyers and educated but disaffected individuals socially above the mass of citizenship but well below the ruling nobility of the Ancien

Régime. Robespierre, for example, was a lawyer, establishing in perhaps the most vivid manner possible the now hoary link between practising law as a profession and being completely unfamiliar with the spirit of justice.

This class factor, of individuals from educated but alienated backgrounds, forms a consistent feature of the most destructive revolutionary movements and still applies today. The leaders of many anticolonial movements were of this disaffected middle-class type, with some in the French colonies of the Far East, for example, having studied in Paris. The most obvious example of this process by which subsequent revolutionaries were inspired by the French Revolution can be seen in the case of Pol Pot, whose leadership killed roughly 25% of the population of Cambodia (between 1.5 and 3 million people out of a population of 8 million). Pol Pot had a typical middle-class revolutionary background as the son of a wealthy farmer educated at elite institutions. In the 1940s, he moved to Paris and joined the French Communist Party. Alongside texts by Stalin and Mao, he enjoyed reading Rousseau and was influenced by an anarchist reading of the French Revolution, Peter Kropotkin's *The Great Revolution*.

Lenin, Trotsky and Mao all shared the same sort of middle-class background as Pol Pot. Lenin was born to a wealthy middle-class family in Simbirsk, and was educated at Kazan Imperial University before being expelled for taking part in anti-Tsarist demonstrations. Trotsky was born to a Ukrainian-Jewish family of wealthy farmers and again was a middle-class intellectual who studied philosophy (he was fluent in several languages including French). Mao was similarly born into a family of wealthy farmers (one might be forgiven for supposing any child of a wealthy farmer between the late 18th and early 20th century to be a potential mass-murdering dictator) and fully radicalised by the time he worked at Peking University. Even England's earlier 'revolutionary', Oliver Cromwell, shared this sort of background, although his own position as a yeoman farmer entailed greater actual poverty than that experienced by leading early Communists.

What we can say is that there is a consistent propensity amongst a certain class of society towards destructive rebellion in the mould of the French Revolution. This background combines a certain degree of education (so that many of those from this class are university educated or have had access to extended schooling, whereby they were exposed to revolutionary texts and radical political ideas) with a psychological or individual leaning towards absolutist solutions. Such people always feel that the existing political structure is fundamentally flawed and requires not just evolution or revision but exists as an impediment to all progress and must therefore be completely destroyed before such progress can occur.

If we look at Cultural Marxists today, we can see that they are still primarily from this same narrow social background and still primarily influenced by the French Revolution. The French Revolution combined the highest of professed ideals with the most barbaric of behaviours, and this template of encoded ideological hypocrisy is still commonplace today. To contemporary Cultural Marxists, only loyalty to the ideology matters; all traditional moral restraints, especially their universal application under the Enlightenment assumption of shared human dignity, are abandoned. Enemies of the ideology lose their rights to free speech, to free thought, to peaceful protest or gathering, to equal employment opportunities, to self-expression in the workplace, or the public sphere, or the university campus, or the television studio, and will even, as these things progress, lose the right to express unsanctioned opinions in the privacy of their own homes (look at the way the private conversations of Trump became major public scandals or the way that private messages shared between friends can end up losing people their jobs if they are ever leaked).

In the French Revolution, we saw the transition from high ideal to savage mob rule. *The Declaration of the Rights of Man and the Citizen* (1789), with its laudable assertion that "Men are born and remain free and equal in rights" contained the seeds of its destruction in the very next line: "Social distinctions may be founded only upon the general good." All well and good until you get to deciding who judges what this vague 'general good' is and how much power they have to adjust 'social distinctions' to fit their preconceived concepts of what that good is. The universal right is immediately contradicted by the issue of who enforces that right and how. In the same fashion, today we see Cultural Marxists assuming absolute power to determine social distinction, and absolute power to use any method they wish to correct 'inequalities' that may be either entirely morally justified, or caused, not by injustice in society, but by their own biased interpretation of it.

The people doing this are nearly always of the same middle-class backgrounds. The working class are far too often possessed of natural conservative instincts, knowing from experience that sensible personal choices have as much effect on personal outcomes as any impositions of wider society. They are not protected from poor personal choices by wealth or contacts, and are engaged far more in the daily struggle of existence and the effort to feed, clothe and sustain themselves. Their concerns are practical rather than ideological, their experience real rather than removed, which is precisely why they see the impact of poor policy choices before the middle and upper classes do. They reject mass immigration, for example, because it is their wages that are depressed by it, and it is their areas which are made more dangerous by increased crime and social alienation.

The utopian promises of the globalist and Cultural Marxist ideologies, the false lure of pretending that there are no cultural differences or strains in infrastructure, are unconvincing to those who live these issues. Only the middle class in general has the luxury of time and comfort required to become ideological revolutionaries intent on dismantling the entire structure of Western civilisation. Only people in that social position are insulated against the negative effects of the ideology they impose. Only when the forces they unleash descend into factionalism, as the Girondins and Dantonists found to their cost during the French Revolution, do these middle-class revolutionaries suffer the consequences of their actions.

16

Anarchism

"Anarchism is founded on the observation that
since few men are wise enough to rule themselves,
even fewer are wise enough to rule others."

—Edward Abbey

THE ONE POSITIVE THAT CAN BE OFFERED FOR
Anarchism is that it is at least an intellectually honest position to hold. As
Western societies move increasingly rapidly towards a sort of 'soft' tyranny
akin to that of contemporary Communist China (allowing capitalism and
personal self-gratification through trivial luxuries in return for a denial of
widespread political engagement), the lure of rejecting all political authority
grows stronger. Whilst often considered a left-wing position (and often being
so), Anarchism can appeal to those on the Right who prioritise individual
liberty even more than natural conservatism does. The Anarchist concept of a
society of voluntary associations can meet the libertarian aspiration towards
small or non-existent government interference in every area of individual
endeavour. In this sense, we can see Anarchism and Libertarianism as two
faces of the same coin, a coin minted on a voluntary exchange rather than
a state-backed one.

Anarchism as a political philosophy unfortunately has not, in its choice of methods and targets, distinguished itself morally from the very structures of government it opposes. Individual Anarchists display the same moral range as individual government officials, but in the 19th century in particular, Anarchism was responsible for a succession of actions that would today be defined as terrorist atrocities. It is also the case that the political philosophy founded on the rejection of authority or, according to the Greek meaning, on being 'one without rulers' must necessarily be a chaotic sort of movement likely to appeal to a very diverse range of actors. An Anarchism that defines itself by the social mores and rules of the society in which it is formed is a self-contradictory beast, as is one that readily accepts any narrow definition of its own aims and methodologies.

The same problem applies to the efforts of more prominent Anarchists to either define the movement accurately or direct the actions of other Anarchists. At what point does such an effort contradict the core assumption of Anarchism itself, which is that one must not be led by others and that all action must be entirely voluntary? Proudhon might have given the thing a name in the mid-19th century, but no true Anarchist would follow some narrow Proudhonist manifesto that contradicted his or her own notions of political freedom.

There are competing historical roots to the central idea of Anarchism, and not all of these are exclusive to Western civilisation. Any rejection of the impositions of the State through history is likely to have some oblique, indirect, but sympathetic relationship to some aspects of Anarchism. In the moment of rebellion, when they take up a banner and march on the streets, however peacefully, or when they refuse to pay a tax or when they deny a government's authority over them, every rebel becomes to some extent an Anarchist. For history tells us that any protest has the power to become a revolution, if it lasts long enough, spreads widely enough, or becomes violent enough (or all three). In practical terms, we call any complete collapse of government or of State cohesion and power "anarchy", before we know what will follow.

In relation to our own topic and the chapters which have preceded this one, we can link Anarchism in its earliest manifestation, many centuries before the term itself existed, to the Greek philosophical debt. In their usual restless intellectual fecundity, the Ancient Greeks did not merely engage themselves with questioning, defining and rebelling against accepted theology and the power of the gods. Secular authority could hardly escape the Greek (especially Athenian) combination of rational enquiry and love of liberty. It was inevitable that if Greeks were prepared to question the existence of the gods, they were also prepared to question the nature of all other forms of power, to question, if you like, the existence of power in every political form. Whilst some, like Plato, would do this by delivering reflections on the nature of statehood and political power by reference to the structure of a mythical society (in *Timaeus* and *Critias*, followed by *The Republic*), others, like Diogenes of Sinope, the living embodiment of the Cynic school of philosophy, would display this questioning by means of personal example.

Diogenes, by manifesting a complete rejection of all conventional morality in his personal behaviour, could be said to have been enacting an ideology that would eventually become Anarchism, and to have done so via what would be called today 'direct action'. Diogenes is said to have slept in a barrel and to have masturbated and defecated freely and in public as a signal of freedom from conventional restraint. Avant-garde artistes of the modern period, as well as unknowing Anarchists squatting (in every sense) in seized flats, would repeat these transgressive gestures throughout the 20th century without the least knowledge of their origins. I can personally recall an English teacher of my youth with an interest in philosophy relating the tale of having witnessed an 'avante-garde' performance of 'art' which consisted of defecating on a stage. Such acts, of course, remind most of us of the benefits as much as the drawbacks of conventional morals.

The distinction between Anarchism and Liberalism is often depicted as an economic one centred on the libertarian desire for personal economic freedoms and the logical extension of these towards others (thereby enabling *laissez-faire* capitalism and freewheeling right-wing economics). However, the distinction could just as easily be drawn in moral terms relating to the kind of direct action undertaken by Diogenes. Whilst both prefer voluntary choice over State direction, the Anarchist often chooses to reject conventional morality alongside State authority, whereas the Libertarian often sees conventional morality as one of the things they voluntarily accept (and that others would voluntarily accept) in the absence of State coercion.

The Anarchist demands the freedom to offend, whilst the Libertarian rejects the offences of the State and its powerful intrusions into individual life. These two things are subtly different, even while they can lead to similar conclusions. It is only when the Anarchist becomes deliberately transgressive, in the moral sense, seeing freedom as the breaking of taboos, that the difference becomes obvious. This, and not economic differences, actually lie behind the differences between the Anarchist and the Libertarian. Too often the Anarchist wishes to impose on others, whilst the Libertarian wishes only not to be imposed upon by others.

These distinctions inform not only what Anarchism is but also how Cultural Marxists respond to it. Cultural Marxists will accept any manifestation of Anarchism that is in the manner of Diogenes, insofar as his behaviour involved the transgression of traditional moral views. This type of Anarchism is entirely compatible with their own project of dismantling the entire structure of Western civilisation and every traditional view that goes with it. Thus, Cultural Marxists will always admire and promote the moral transgression of Western societal taboos. Doing so accelerates the collapse of Western civilisation that they impatiently await. Whether it is the Romantic or Gothic artistic sensibility of moral rebellion (prevalent in art from Byron onwards) or academic justifications of various behaviours once considered perverse (especially in LGBT activism), the Cultural Marxist will always delight in the breaking of established Western taboos. The Cultural Marxist attitude to purely political Anarchism will, however, be far more complicated, and somewhat typically far more hypocritical and selective too.

We can see this by reference to three recent movements or events and the Cultural Marxist responses to them. These three movements are alternative media, online hacking and information release, and the Yellow Vests in France (who, as I write, are entering their ninth week of mass protest). All three are movements that would be celebrated by those who genuinely oppose State power, who genuinely wish to see conventional wisdom challenged, or who genuinely adhere to either Anarchist or Libertarian principles of protest and freedom. All three directly challenge political authority and genuinely come from a wellspring of public political discontent with some well-justified grievances. Any Anarchist would delight in all three as a potential fulfilment of William Godwin's belief that the imposition of State authority would naturally wither away following a process of (largely) peaceful political evolution. Whilst Godwin, in *Political Justice* (1793), might not have provided much prior support for the kind of revolutionary action undertaken by the Yellow Vests, the purely verbal and written rebellions of the first two movements are surely consistent with a peaceful Anarchist solution to overbearing State power.

With alternative media, the response of Cultural Marxism has universally been to condemn the democratisation of commentary occasioned via the Internet, social media and independent news sources. This is because, of course, professional news services have long since abandoned all journalistic integrity and any desire to present news in a factual and objective manner. Outlets such as the BBC are of course part of the apparatus of the State, dependent on coerced funding from a populace increasingly alienated from the orthodox political stances propagated by these news sources. Alternative media has arisen as an alternative, not because the general public or those who seek out these newer voices are more susceptible to 'fake news' than others, but because they are LESS susceptible to the fake news and increasingly obvious partisan bias of mainstream news sources. Rather as Katie Hopkins pointed out to Ian Hislop with reference to her 'shocking' public pronouncements, alternative media is the 'monster' created by the arrogance, the corruption and the social experimentation of the mainstream media.

People have been forced by mainstream failures to look for and support alternatives precisely because the mainstream media don't even know themselves when they are lying anymore. Their bias is inescapable unless one goes to a different provider. Nor is it the acceptable bias of a group that declares its interest. The mainstream media, while being more relentlessly partisan than they have ever been before, still insist that they are the objective arbiters of truth, that they are professionally impartial. This, whilst producing a slew of articles every day comparing an elected US President who, in office, has assiduously followed every law of the American Republic to a genocidal Nazi maniac who broke every law of the Weimar Republic in order to assume office.

Independent news sources, from Breitbart to Rebel Media or independent, self-promoting commentators like Paul Joseph Watson are increasingly in danger of actual imprisonment for expressing views the globalist, Cultural Marxist establishment dislikes. Cultural Marxists in power have increased, via selective hate speech legislation and via liberal dominated social media platforms, the threat to free speech and free thought in the West to levels not seen since Eastern Europe was under the Communist yoke and not seen in France, Spain or Germany since genuine fascists were in power.

Just recently in Britain, with the arrest of James Goddard (a self declared British Yellow Vest), we have seen the grotesque spectacle of a British citizen being arrested for the crime of peacefully criticising an MP. Goddard offered no violence but only called the MP a "Nazi", an insult which, whilst false, has been employed regularly by Cultural Marxists in power themselves. All alternative narratives, as well as alternative news sources, are potentially criminal in a society which has lost all respect for free speech. A Richard Reich in the US can call Trump a "Nazi" with impunity. Cultural Marxists in the UK can deploy similar slurs targeted at a Nigel Farage, a Jacob Rees-Mogg, or any working class pro-Brexit protestor. The Speaker of the House, of course, does not write letters to the head of the Metropolitan Police demanding that he himself or Anna Soubry be arrested for 'hate speech' or 'public disorder' when employing the exact same language about millions of Leave voters that James Goddard had used about Anna Soubry.

If, of course, Cultural Marxists were Anarchists or Libertarians, they would be on the side of these alternative voices. But they are not. They are natural authoritarians and totalitarians, eager for the agents of the State to crush all dissent and delighted when they do so. They vigorously advocate for the criminalisation of political opinions which diverge from their own. Nor are they usually in the weaker position in such contests. Thanks to the long march through the institutions they have undertaken over the last fifty years, thanks to their embedded place in key institutions of government and media (deliberately increased by groups like Common Purpose), they can now direct official power against their political enemies. The institutions that should defend the foundation stone of Western political life (free speech) are the very institutions being used to destroy it. Without the capacity to criticise those in power free of the fear of politically motivated reprisals, there is no means to hold power to account or to preserve democracy when it is threatened by other actions of the ruling class.

The totalitarian nature of Cultural Marxism is again displayed in its reaction to the anarchistic direct action of hackers and disseminators of State secrets. The most famous examples here are the hacktivist group Anonymous and Wikileaks, formed by longtime hacker Julian Assange. Wikileaks famously released a huge quantity of US government files in a series of 'informational attacks' on US power and policy, the most notorious being a tranche of secret files supplied by Chelsea Manning in 2010. Anonymous was formed in 2004 as a voluntary collective of hackers who were users of the alternative imageboard website 4chan (itself a key spawning ground of anarchistic and alternative voices critiquing the Cultural Marxist consensus. Such online phenomena as Pepe memes, Kekistani memes, and more recent NPC memes flourish on 4chan subcultures). Anonymous have targeted several governments and institutions with coordinated hacking attacks, including Western governments as well as terrorist organisations.

Both Assange and Anonymous are interesting for following through on the core logic of Anarchism. Both have been indiscriminate in their targeting of organisations and nation states, having released information relating both to Western powers and their established enemies. In this sense, they have been consistent with Anarchistic principles, possessing no 'master'. But in applying themselves wherever they perceive deception or oppression, they have acted in ways that horrify Cultural Marxists. When Assange was releasing confidential US government military secrets, he was a fêted hero of the Left and of Cultural Marxism generally (a rare instance in some ways, however, of the 'establishment' Cultural Marxists and the 'street' Cultural Marxists being opposed). As soon as Assange decided that the same logic of resistance applied to senior members of the Democratic Party as well as their Presidential candidate, former supporters turned against him. He had made the mistake of targeting someone Cultural Marxists needed in power to fulfil their agenda. A similar Cultural Marxist waning of enthusiasm occurred when Anonymous proved that they were prepared to hack the Left as well as the Right.

Together with the voluntary hacking associations online, the Yellow Vest movement is perhaps the purest expression of Anarchism in the West today. It has no universally acknowledged leaders. Its gatherings and marches have been organised in a minimal, "flash mob" style online or by text, or otherwise have been purely spontaneous expressions of collective dissent. It is not tied to any particular party and has a multiplicity of aims and actors. It has been the Western European equivalent of the Arab Spring, though notably far less welcome to Western European leaders. It directly challenges the authority of one of the leading globalists of the EU, French Premier Macron, who had himself taken power by deploying a populist surge he never intended to honour once in power. Macron, remember, was supposed to be the leader of a new movement, an alternative to the corrupt old parties of Left and Right. The realisation that neither he nor his movement were such an alternative, but rather a sleight of hand by which another globalist who did not care for France nor the French was placed in charge, is a major spur to the protests against him.

As stated above, as I write this it is now the ninth week of Yellow Vest protests in France. For nine weeks, there has been protesting which has struck scores of cities and involved in the course of that time hundreds of thousands (at least) of participants. Macron's approval rating has slumped to just 20%, less than half of that enjoyed by President Trump. But compare the media coverage. Every ten minutes, we are told that Trump's presidency is in crisis, that Trump is an unbalanced maniac, and that Trump is universally despised. We have not once been told similar things of Macron, except by the kind of independent commentators that Cultural Marxists are constantly trying to silence. The mainstream media has not criticised Macron once, whilst his people have been in open revolt for more than two months.

I have personally seen perhaps one report on mainstream television media about the Yellow Vests, loaded with the pejorative language always deployed by the mainstream media of challenges to Cultural Marxists in power. Macron has made his own Cultural Marxist credentials clear, which is precisely why the people dislike him and the media won't report that dislike or criticise him themselves. Macron opined that there is no such thing as French culture. He has referred to protestors exercising their democratic rights as "extremists" and "racists", calling them "xenophobes" and "uneducated" (standard Cultural Marxist *ad hominems*). Just before the protests, he gave a speech almost identical to one by German leader Angela Merkel, both of which deployed the standard Cultural Marxist tactic of redefining the meaning of words to suit their own agenda. Macron told us that nationalism was the opposite of patriotism. Nationalism was evil and inevitably destined for the dustbin of history. The patriots were those who supported globalist institutions, rule by the (unelected) EU, and open borders. As ever, the truly frightening part is that he probably believes it.

The lack of reporting on a massive scale of protest in one of the leading EU nations testifies to the Cultural Marxist domination of mainstream media. Macron has expressed support for the ideology they share. Therefore criticism of Macron is silenced. I check the British news quite regularly. Along with a single TV report, I can think of only two newspaper articles from mainstream sources, both of which told me how dreadful the protests (and protestors) were. The only way you will see the crowds of thousands protesting in multiple cities is via alternative media. France burns, night after night, and nothing on our media. And this occurs whilst that same media is telling us, in report after report, that EU membership secures stability, economic wellbeing, peace and social harmony. Events which prove the opposite are occurring as they report on warnings that are future fantasies regarding the dangers of Brexit. France burns, and to the BBC, ITV, C4, to the readers of the Daily Mail or The Guardian, to those who write or work for all mainstream outlets as well as those who rely exclusively on them, it is as if it is not happening. The flames are invisible. This cannot be coincidental. This cannot be an accidental lapse of reporting. I'm sure someone really determined to can find a few reports, but anything like the attention it deserves? I think not. You are not supposed to hear, or care. More especially, you are not supposed to compare. Don't compare this lack of reporting to the excessive reporting of horrors which have not happened and are purely speculative propaganda regarding Brexit.

Think also of the actions of the French government in response to the Yellow Vest protests. Macron has deployed snipers on the rooftops of Paris and elsewhere. Jackbooted and aggressive police in huge numbers have been deployed, and protestors have been beaten on multiple occasions. Draconian new laws are proposed to ban all Yellow Vest protests. Imagine if Trump did the same thing to anti-Trump protestors. Imagine if Trump arrested people for wearing a pink pussy hat, in the way that people in France are being arrested for wearing a yellow jacket. Imagine if Trump had someone arrested for calling him a "Nazi", the way Speaker Bercow and MP Anna Soubry had British Yellow Vest James Goddard arrested. Consider that this heavy-handed response of French authorities is by no means unique among modern EU governments. The same has occurred to Yellow Vests in Belgium.

The Yellow Vest movement is also not the first time we have seen supposed liberal democracies in Europe, which make much of their tolerance, openness and democracy, brutally repressing protest. The same occurred to Catalan referendum voters brutalised by the Spanish police and to elected Catalan leaders arbitrarily removed from power in 2017. 92% of voters voted for independence from Spain. Only 7% voted against independence. Most of the Catalan leaders were arrested and the result ignored and declared illegal by the Spanish authorities, with the full support of the EU. Consider that Macron today and the Spanish in 2017 have not responded any differently to public uprisings against their governments to the way the Chinese Communists responded to the Tiananmen Square uprising of 1989. What is there to distinguish the uprisings in France or Spain from any previous uprising against tyranny? What is there to distinguish the official responses of EU governments from those of actual tyrannies?

And for a Britain that does not obtain the Brexit it voted for, as seems increasingly likely, what is there to stop us facing, in future protests, the same police snipers or the same complicit media silence? When democracies confer power to unelected bodies, and ignore democratic votes, how are they, any more, democracies? As yet, Cultural Marxists are not using State or supra-national power to directly murder political dissidents, as, say, the Soviet Union or the Chinese Communist Party did. But the difference here is one of degree, not kind, for Cultural Marxists are already making dissent itself, as public protest, as information release, as unofficial reportage, and even as mild heckling on a public street, a criminal matter. They are already arresting political dissidents on trumped up charges, in a supposedly free Europe. It is as yet a softer tyranny than many of the past, but it is still a tyranny, and nothing like the democracy we were born with.

17

THE RUSSIAN REVOLUTION & COMMUNISM

*"The Russian revolution was to an unprecedented
degree the cause of the proletariat of the whole
world becoming more revolutionary."*

—Karl Liebknecht

THE INFLUENCE OF COMMUNISM AND THE RUSSIAN
Revolution on Cultural Marxism should be relatively self-evident, so this
precursor of Cultural Marxist thinking requires less exposition than for
other influences. It is still necessary, however, to make the similarities as
plain as we can.

The two main lessons which Cultural Marxism draws from Communism,
ideologically, are a simplistic hatred of capitalism, business and the ordinary
economic stratagems of Western nations, and a deterministic historical sense
that society is inevitably moving in their direction. Just as Communists
believe that the internal logic of the inequalities of capitalism lead to its
inevitable replacement by Communism, so, too, do Cultural Marxists firmly
believe that their thinking is the thinking of the future and is destined to
supplant all alternatives. They are, after all, 'progressives'. Humanity is inevitably, in their eyes, travelling in the political direction of their choice.

Some of the brutality of Cultural Marxist thought derives from impatience with those who would deny this historical determinism or seek to slow the process by which Cultural Marxism replaces traditional Western values. To Cultural Marxists, such resistance is, as the Borg would put it, futile, and therefore unnecessarily wasteful and selfish. Any casualties in the path of this determined future are consequently the fault of those who resist Cultural Marxism, not of Cultural Marxism itself. This accords entirely with Stalinist, Maoist or classical Communist attitudes to the deaths and atrocities they have been actually responsible for. The victims, or some other group that placed the victims between the Communist and the Communist utopia to come, were guilty, not the Communists themselves.

An ideological conviction of inevitable triumph excuses any brutality committed to hasten that triumph, as does the utopian assurance that the future perfect society, once reached, will justify any steps taken to reach it. As yet, of course, Cultural Marxism has not piled up the impressive number of corpses that Communism used as a bridge of bodies towards the perfect future, but there is little to suggest that it would not follow such an example given the power to do so. Cultural Marxists already endorse the kind of political thuggery with which both Nazism and Communism commenced, and have already excused political murders committed by allies together with street violence, rioting, looting, arbitrary arrests, online harassment, doxxing and various social exclusions on political grounds. They already possess both the requisite utopianism and authoritarianism to take the path of violence, and to justify every step along it to themselves.

It is because of this sense of inevitable triumph, this inherited Communist historical determinism, that Cultural Marxists often refer to themselves as "progressives" and as everything they seek to attain as "social progress". Every act is part of a progression towards their utopia, no matter how destructive that act is by traditional moral judgement. A central irony, of course, is that Cultural Marxism is actually as out-dated as modernism is as an artistic movement. Cultural Marxists' sense of their own modernity and their assurance that they represent a coming future are themselves rather ancient concepts, similar to fanatical religious notions of "mission" or nationalist expressions of "manifest destiny". At the very least, these feelings are held in common with Communism itself, and therefore currently just over a century old. Cultural Marxism is thus a modern manifestation of old and failed ideas rather than something genuinely innovative. Its notions of what progress is are defined by ancient injustices which it obsessively picks at whilst ignorant of more recent examples, including those which it is itself responsible for. Even the lexicon it deploys references past struggles rather than present realities, labelling by terms such as "imperialist" or "fascist" things which are in fact neither imperial nor fascistic.

As the KGB defector Yuri Bezmonov indicated, most of the aims of Communism and Cultural Marxism are identical, and the primary target is the destruction of Western civilisation. It is the methodology which differs, and the regional concentration, rather than the intentions behind the movement. Cultural Marxism is internationalist and embedded within the cultures it opposes, rather than geographically centred in some rival nation or collection of nations. It is an enemy already within the walls. Communism itself, however, was important in providing two things in the early days of Cultural Marxism. First, it provided the validating example of success that assured Cultural Marxists that Western civilisation could be toppled, just as the Tsarist or Imperial Chinese regimes had been toppled by Communism. The psychological importance of such a valid, real world example was enormous in terms of cementing Cultural Marxist self-belief and a willingness to undertake the kind of lifetime struggle required to force established and relatively secure societies towards major cultural shifts in direction.

Second, as Bezmonov also attested, Communism and existing Communist regimes provided practical assistance to Cultural Marxist individuals and groups. Professional validation, financial contributions, logistical support, tactical advice and more flowed from Soviet agents towards prominent Cultural Marxist individuals. Whilst never controlling the related ideology as a whole, the Soviets could and did provide necessary assistance where required. Since the fall of Soviet Communism, we have seen this supportive role adopted by Islam, which again, just like the USSR, is happy to exploit a growing Western tendency to attack itself. This is especially evident in the sphere of media propaganda, a prime example being Qatari funding of the media channel AJ+, which produces a constant stream of Cultural Marxist content. Islam's willingness to take on the role of belligerent "other" to Western civilisation, and some Islamic nations' willingness to fund Cultural Marxist outlets, saved Cultural Marxism itself from collapse in the wake of the loss of Soviet support.

In attitudes towards Soviet history, the Cultural Marxist will also reveal his or her own nature. Cultural Marxists will still downplay Communist atrocities. They will see the utopian aims of Communism as far more signifi-cant than the crimes. They will be unable to recognise the brutal associations of Communist imagery, symbology and rhetoric, and will often deploy these themselves with no consciousness that doing so is similar in any way to Nazi regalia (by which they will be horrified). Whilst obsessed with fictional infringements of good manners causing offence to them, such as imaginary micro-aggressions, facial expressions possessed of a meaning only they discern, and even mild patriotic imagery not associated with violent regimes, they will consider displays of Communist iconography to be either worthy or amusing, at worst ironic statements that cannot offend others.

A beautiful illustration of this came when Jordan Peterson was inter-viewed by a young Cultural Marxist whose clipboard was emblazoned with a Communist hammer and sickle. Peterson's refusal to use newly invented pronouns was considered by this interviewer to be plainly more offensive than a symbol associated with 100 million deaths. When Peterson correctly mentioned the historical context of the Communist symbol, the result was bewildered amusement.

18

ANTI-COLONIALISM

"You cannot continue to victimize someone else just because you yourself were a victim once — there has to be a limit."

—Edward Said

AT THE HEIGHT OF BRITISH IMPERIAL POWER, history witnessed one of the most remarkable military endeavours of all time, in an event the details of which are not taught, as far as I know, in any British school today. In its own time, however, the British Abyssinian Campaign of 1868 was celebrated as one of the most incredible triumphs of British military might the world had witnessed, and was considered to have provided an instructive lesson to all other nations of both the unassailability of British power and the terrible consequences of spurning it.

The Abyssinian Campaign was the result of rash actions on the part of the Abyssinian Emperor Tewodros (or Theodore) II, who was keen to assert his authority in the face of multiple internal threats within the large territories he ruled in what is now Ethiopia. Despite ruling an ancient and once powerful realm (covering a geographical territory far more extensive than that of the British isles), Theodore, a Christian ruler who claimed descent from the biblical Solomon, was faced with both expansionism from external Islamic tribes and internal revolt from his own populace. Deciding that external allies would be beneficial, he sought assistance from European powers to modernise and pacify his nation.

Whilst this in itself was probably a sensible policy, he had the misfortune of not being able to offer much significant benefit in return. Letters to the French, Prussians, Austrians and Russians went unanswered, as did a supplication addressed to Queen Victoria. Theodore misread the international situation by appealing to Western nations as fellow Christians, a move that might have endeared him to missionaries but in no way made the weak Abyssinia a more attractive regional partner than the Muslim Ottoman Empire, which the British, the most powerful international players of all, saw as a check on Russian expansionism and as an important supplier, through Egypt, of the cotton needed for the British textile trade.

Following the rebuff of receiving no replies to his solicitations for aid, Theodore turned initial disinterest into active opposition by the disastrous decision to arrest and detain a British missionary, Henry Stern. Stern had made the mistake of seemingly disputing the Emperor's claimed descent with a reference to his humble origins. Despite a generally flattering tone overall, his commentary enraged the already disappointed Theodore, who perhaps saw it as undermining his authority yet further. Stern and his porters and assistants were arrested, subjected to multiple beatings and imprisoned in the Emperor's own palace. Efforts from the British Consul, Charles Duncan Cameron, and others failed to secure the release of the prisoners, and by contrast seemed to provoke growing paranoia and hostility from the Emperor in response to foreign pressure upon him. The British then took the decision to mount a rescue effort to militarily secure Stern's release.

Even in the 1860's, such a decision was noteworthy. Today, we can be assured, no such military response would greet the abduction of a single British citizen by any other power, even after diplomatic efforts had failed. Whilst it is common for Western powers to try to secure release of those captured by other nations or criminal or terrorist groups, they do not make massive commitments of resources in defence of a single life or of the princi-ple that citizenship imparts global protection to any extent needed. Military interventions are in the first instance usually about evacuating threatened citizens before they are captured by advancing hostile groups, not about engaging in punishment or rescue missions. Even when the Iranians captured 15 Royal Navy personnel in 2007, the British response was purely diplo-matic (it takes such actions to actually be on British soil, as with the Iranian Embassy siege of 1980, for more forceful responses).

But the Abyssinian Expedition of 1868 is instructive of our general theme not only in showing the difference in imperial and post-imperial strategic responses. It is also telling regarding the relative global power such responses reveal and the cultural confidence underlying that power. For the British expedition under General Napier was not really comparable to an embassy siege or the deployment of handfuls of highly trained special forces. It was a full-blown invasion of another nation. The Expedition consisted of 13,000 troops and 26,000 camp followers. It included forty-four trained elephants sent from India to pull siege equipment. The British built a new railway with twenty miles of track to transport supplies from the coast. 40,000 pack animals, primarily mules and horses, were required to transport the supplies further. A 700-yard-long pier with steel supports was built. The main body of troops embarked from Bombay in 280 sailing vessels. An advance party of engineers built a 63-mile road rising to 7,400 feet into hilly badlands. The Expedition took three months to laboriously trek through inhospitable terrain to reach the Abyssinian fortress of Magdala.

Nor were the distances involved or building work required the only significant bar to success. The terrain covered included mountain ranges and a huge desert, and the logistics involved were as complex or more so than Hannibal's crossing of the Alps. All of this, remember, because one otherwise entirely obscure British missionary had been beaten and imprisoned. After a short battle and a successful storming of Magdala by the British forces,

Theodore committed suicide. An Emperor had been humbled and forced into suicide, a desert crossed and a nation conquered for the sake of one captured missionary. The imperial message was that Britain's power was so overwhelming that less significant nations could simply not afford any action that might provoke British ire. The lesson was reinforced in an adjoining region after the death of Gordon of Khartoum in 1885, when Kitchener destroyed the Mahdi's fundamentalist nation at the Battle of Omdurman in 1898. In 1896, the shortest recorded war in history, the Anglo-Zanzibar War, which lasted between 38 and 45 minutes, gave the exact same lesson elsewhere.

To fully realise the significance of these largely forgotten Victorian imperial conflicts for the topic of Cultural Marxism, one must be aware of the amount of borrowing from anti-imperial rhetoric of the last century that is made by contemporary Cultural Marxists today. We must also realise how short a time passed, in the grand scheme of things, between the apogee of European imperial power and its complete extinction. Nobody reading the reports of the stunning success of Napier's military adventure in 1868 could have possibly conceived that within a century, most British imperial possessions would have claimed their independence. A child born in the year that saw forty-four elephants and 13,000 troops dispatched from Bombay to defend one British traveller on another continent could possibly have lived long enough to see the Raj end in 1945. Most of the West in the mid-19th century had no real inkling that the scramble for colonial acquisition would relatively swiftly be followed by colonial retreat, nor could they have conceived that almost universal admiration for imperial exploits would give way to the kind of embarrassment or hatred of our former conquests so prevalent today. Both the practical power to intervene and the cultural confidence to do so have departed.

Ironically, of course, this pragmatic and cultural shift has not been reflected entirely in foreign policy. For their own reasons, globalist liberals are as interventionist, if not more so, than their imperial precursors. The difference is that these modern interventions are not backed up by the kind of logistical competence or cultural self-belief shown by Victorians like Napier. Contemporary interventionists are often themselves believers in Cultural Marxism and ignorant of the lessons that could be drawn from Victorian conflicts (let alone from Classical antiquity, which they also despise and are ignorant of). This is an un-admitted reason for the failure to plan interventions properly, which has marked disastrous recent engagements in the Middle East.

If we take the Second Iraq War, Afghanistan, Syria and Libya we see forms of military intervention in foreign conflict which have been ordered by those with absolutely no knowledge of history. The nature of Afghanistan as a region of internecine and unending local feuds which will always have the potential to bog down far superior armed forces than those locally deployed should have been obvious to anyone who had witnessed the Soviet engagement there from 1979 to 1989, let alone anyone who had studied or at least been peripherally aware of the First Anglo-Afghan War of 1838-1842. A student of history with an objective understanding of our colonial past would be able to contrast why that conflict was a disaster and Napier's expedition a triumph, and apply these lessons to interventions today. But, blinded by the idea that all colonial history is a simple tale of oppression Cultural Marxists are unable to draw on such knowledge. It is all 'evil'. It is all 'our colonial guilt'. It is 'a great crime'. Meaning, of course, that the nuances and realities (say the level of internal dissent against Theodore which aided the British) cannot be applied to future decision making. The US for example could have avoided the disaster of Vietnam if they had properly studied the late colonial defeats of the French from whom they ultimately inherited the conflict. But even the most hawkishly conservative US voices considered colonial history an alien territory with no lessons to impart, and themselves as morally superior to it.

Both morally and practically, there is a strong argument to be made that globalism has been more damaging to many communities than imperialism has, and that contemporary financial markets or military adventures are just as prone to immorality, short-sightedness and selfishness as the trading companies that gave economic impetus to colonial expansion. Certainly, many imperial administrators, particularly in the late period of European colonialism, had more moral individual virtues and more coherent policies than politicians or administrators today possess. A Blair or a Trudeau will apologise for imperial 'crimes' of the distant past. But how many hundreds of thousands have died in the Middle East, thanks to policies these politicians supported, and how many thousands in the West have suffered equally, thanks to people these same politicians have imported? The sheer idiocy of building hatred by bombing foreign nations and then importing millions who might possess that hatred, out of a useless 'compassion' that did not stop you bombing in the first place is a uniquely Cultural Marxist moral absurdity.

19

THE DECONSTRUCTION
OF THE WEST

*"...since texts have no objective univocal meaning, I feel
sure that when I call you a bunch of moronic cunts you
will be able to decode that sequence of sequential signifiers
with the appropriate emancipated subjectivity."*

—Jonathan Lynn, *Mayday*

TO THE VAST MAJORITY OF PEOPLE, NAMES LIKE
Derrida, Lacan, Foucault, Barthes, Baudrillard or Deleuze remain merci-
fully obscure. Unless a person has attended university and undertaken a
humanities course, they are unlikely to encounter the texts and ideas of these
figures of post-structuralist criticism in any direct way. But indirectly, they
will find that the entire nature of political and ethical discourse in the West
has been shaped by a number of primarily French academics who came to
prominence within academic circles in the 1960s and 1970s. These figures
were themselves following on from the structuralists of the 1950s, directly
critiquing structuralist assumptions but adopting much of the methodology
and lexicon of the earlier movement to do so.

The structuralists argued that human freedom and choice were essentially illusory, as many of the things we consciously suppose to be choices

are in fact influenced by underlying structures. For some, these might be consequent on brain structure or psychology, for others they are more the result of cultural anthropology, but in both cases, seemingly distinct social organisations and individual choices should not be considered in isolation but as part of a network of hidden exchanges. Different social organisations could in fact be understood as manifestations of the same structures conditioning behavioural responses. Our choices are already set by these structures before we make them. Texts could be understood as manifestations of a set of rules underlying whatever surface topic they embodied, whether those rules were ones of narrative structure, genre or some other series of connections with other texts.

Structuralists are engaged in the task of detecting and defining these systems or rules, being more interested in these structural issues than in surface subject or meaning. As such, they could be seen as the end point of the Enlightenment interest in systemisation and classification, just as a scientist examining atoms could be said to have inherited the thought of the Greek philosophers who postulated the existence of such things long before the invention of the devices which confirmed them.

The post-structuralists differed in terms of their attitude to these structures. Like the structuralists, they prioritised links and connections, often hidden, over reactions to individual works. Like the structuralists they accepted much of the language and thought of the discipline of linguistics, prioritising study of the operation of language itself in any human exchanges. But where the structuralist search for hidden systems lent itself to a belief that everything was explicable and all these connections could be rationally and logically understood, post-structuralists tended to argue that these interplays of structure were just as illusory, in a way, as the surface meanings they had replaced. If anything could be understood, not as itself but as a system of rules between interconnected things, then the operation of these rules was at play, always changing, always escaping complete understanding, always allowing fundamentally different interpretations. Nobody could ever arbitrate which of these structures was real and which was false. Anyone attempting to do so was merely imposing their power, in an act of egoism, which ironically was still a choice made for them by the play of connections.

All of this might seem like nothing other than a branch of philosophy, influenced by linguistics, allowing a small set of people opportunities for infinite navel-gazing. And it is. There is no real practical or societal worth to any structuralist or post-structuralist text. Both represent a point at which the old classical enquiries divert into fruitless and even intellectually masturbatory dead ends. Philosophy in the Greek sense was remarkably utilitarian compared with contemporary philosophy or intellectualism generally. Archimedes was representative rather than unique, with nearly every major Greek philosopher being an inventor and a proto-scientist as well as a teacher, student and scholar. The abstract speculation always had a purpose, whether that was in terms of developing the engineering or mechanical insights required for actual inventions or whether it meant finding the ideas that would improve the philosopher as an individual or society as a whole.

There is no such utility in much contemporary philosophising, which, thanks to a restriction to institutionalised academia, is more about advancing a career of no utility to others than about applying insights for personal or societal improvement. Ancient philosophy tried to make complex experience coherent and to be accessible to all. Contemporary philosophy, particularly the kind dominant in linguistics and literature studies such as that of Derrida, deliberately obfuscates and alienates. Socrates simplified his language and even adopted the persona of a fool to ask the most fundamental questions, hoping that this method would illustrate the falsehood of much established thought. Contemporary philosophers riddle their arguments with self-invented jargon and technicalities, hoping to prove their ideological stances by the impenetrability of their own discourse.

Of course, the life of the mind can and should be valued in and of itself. There is nothing wrong with learning for pleasure, or studying or speculating for the sheer enjoyment it supplies. Only the crassest person would dispute the pleasure to be had from reading and learning for its own sake. On such terms, there would be nothing wrong with contemporary academia or with the deliberately impenetrable gibberish that passes for intellectual enquiry in most university departments. Those who enjoy it could pay for its existence. If someone enjoys trying to read Derrida, I may not understand the pleasure but I have no right to curtail it.

The trouble is that we are not talking about an obscure private pleasure. Almost nobody encounters Derrida because they want to or seek him out. They are required to by syllabus, and an enormous real structure of public funding supports that. Throughout the Western world, billions of pounds of funding flow into higher education. Students and tutors demand that others pay for their entirely non-utilitarian activities. Society in turn has a right to ask if others should indeed foot that bill, and to examine such things as post-structuralist criticism and their social consequences.

What is the actual social effect of the lessons contained within post-structuralism? The greatest and most damaging is the intellectual validation and pervasive spread of moral and cultural relativism. Post-structuralism and Cultural Marxism are not one and the same, but each feeds upon and supports the other. They are symbiotic. We can see this if we present post-structuralist critical assumptions and Cultural Marxist political assumptions side by side:

Post-Structuralism	Cultural Marxism
The Western Canon exists not because of qualitative excellence but because Westerners are structurally conditioned to value these works	Western literature and art is no more advanced than any other culture.

Civilisation does not reference objective achievements. It references arbitrary value judgements.	Western Civilisation is not civilised. It's actually more barbaric than other cultures.
Western texts exist to be studied to reveal flaws in Western thinking.	Western thinking is fundamentally flawed.
Insanity and madness are cultural value judgements rather than clinical realities. They are about the operation of power (Foucault).	Policies that seem insane to traditionalists are actually the most progressive and worthwhile.
Language always escapes the meanings we seek to impose upon it (Derrida).	Words can mean whatever they need to mean, to support Cultural Marxist positions.
In order to illustrate how language operates, we play with meanings and subvert the expectation that our ideas should make sense.	Our ideas do not need to make sense. They only need to 'feel' right.
Logic, Reason and Evidence are all subjective. They are cultural movements or ideas rather than objective truths.	Our ideas do not need to be logical, rational or provide any concrete evidence. They are just true.

From these similarities, we can see how ideas which might hold some partial truths if limited to textual analysis become devastating socially when enacted as political truths. Everything unique to Western civilisation is debased and devalued, or in the language of post-structuralism, decoded and deconstructed. Of course, Western civilisation has always been created and enacted by fallible human beings. We should not see it as either infallible or unquestionable. But it is objectively true, by any analysis of technological or scientific discovery or any fair analysis of history, that Western civilisation has contributed more good to the world than bad, and more to the standards of living we today enjoy than any other culture.

The problem with the moral relativism inspired by the post-structuralist assumption that everything is subjective and there is no actual objectivity or truth anywhere is that it allows the dishonesties and anti-Western bias of

Cultural Marxism an intellectual space in which to thrive. And via universities and their role in spreading these ideas, we pay for our own cultural destruction. Just as the French Revolution had an enormous impact on the justification for violent revolt against traditional Western society, so too has the French intellectual revolution of the mid-twentieth century had an enormous impact on the undermining of Western heritage and achievement by the very bodies once entrusted with the custodianship of that cultural legacy.

Cultural Marxists use academia to teach a hatred of Western society, history, literature and culture; post-structuralist criticism and its denial of logic, reason and other traditional modes of enquiry facilitates that. This is even before we turn to the actual political pronouncements of many of these critics, which are even more directly engaged in undermining Western values. An academic who tells us that there is nothing more beautiful than a car on fire does potentially as much damage to society as the rioter who sets it alight.

20

THE FRANKFURT SCHOOL

*"What can oppose the decline of the West is not a
resurrected culture but the utopia that is silently
contained in the image of its decline."*

—Theodor W. Adorno

THE FRANKFURT SCHOOL IS A SPECIFIC EXAMPLE

of an academic movement influential throughout the periods of both
Structuralism and Post-Structuralism. It is impossible to present a book on
Cultural Marxism without mentioning at least briefly what the Frankfurt
School was and is, just as it might be impossible to write a history of Spanish
football without mentioning Real Madrid. To extend that analogy, structuralism and post-modernism/post-structuralism can be understood as styles
of playing football, whereas the Frankfurt School is better understood as a
famous club linked to those styles.

As with the dependence of Marx on the generosity of Engels and his
inherited wealth, and as with the largely middle- and upper-class nature of
committed Marxism in the West, the Frankfurt School was made possible
with inherited capitalist wealth. In 1923, Frank Weil, heir to a fortune his
father Herman had made exporting grain from Argentina to Europe, used
his wealth to found an institute dedicated to the study of German society

via Marxist readings of history, sociology and economics. This Institute for Social Research was initially attached to Goethe University Frankfurt, but was closed in 1933 by the Nazis and re-established at Columbia University in New York during a period in which many European intellectuals and academics made their way to the US.

From that point on, the Frankfurt School's explicitly Marxist readings, which inevitably tended towards a negative and hostile attitude towards European peoples and nation states as well as aspects of the US that had inherited defining traditional characteristics from these, were hugely influential on academia across a range of disciplines. Academics such as Max Horkheimer, Theodor Adorno, Herbert Marcuse, Friedrich Pollock, Walter Benjamin, and Eric Fromm shaped intellectual enquiry to the dictates of Marxist propaganda, perhaps forever poisoning any conception of genuine scholarly objectivity. By the time of Jurgen Habermas, the thinking behind the Frankfurt School had become a global academic mindset, influential in every single discipline of the humanities and social sciences and increasingly bringing the academic world into direct political opposition to the inherited values of Western civilisation.

As with our discussion of the post-structuralists, much of this academic history might seem like a deflection from the important world of political events. After all, the idea of the ivory tower academic divorced from reality is not a cliché that emerged out of nowhere, but one reflective of the genuine lack of contact between most ordinary citizens and tenured academics. Nor are academics, even the most successful, generally the most rewarded and privileged people in our society. Academic pay is reasonable, but by no means spectacular, and sales of academic tomes rarely trouble the bestseller lists. Most people will never hear anything about these academics, never encounter them in their daily lives, and never realise the extent to which their prejudices and assumptions have shaped the world we live in. Because these cerebral toilers of the elite class, with far less fame, acclaim or resources than successful actors, comedians, musicians and sportsmen, shape the world like worms shape soil.

Take for example just one work of the highly productive Frankfurt School, famous in its day, which whilst almost unknown to the current general populace, seized the battlefield of culture for the Left in ways that have never been adequately challenged. The Authoritarian Personality, published in 1950, was co-authored by Theodor Adorno, Else Frankel-Brunswick, Daniel Levinson and Nevitt Sanford. All were at that time researchers at the University of California, Berkeley. This book defined an authoritarian personality, the kind of personality one might find in brutal dictators or their thuggish supporters, by nine characteristics on an 'F' scale (for fascism). The characteristics were taken as somehow authoritative or scientific, as objective criteria backed by evidence, but actually reflected the prejudices of the authors more than any meaningful analysis.

Aggressiveness, for example, was defined as an inherently right-wing quality, but then so was 'submission'. The aggressiveness of the Hard Left, the higher death toll of Communist regimes, or the 'submission' inherent to Islamic culture, were all largely ignored in pursuit of the idea that every conservative, patriot or traditionalist was a psychic doppelganger of Adolf Hitler, a recreation in miniature of a unique maniac. Perfectly normal conservative reactions, like a preference for conventional morality on family life or on sexual matters, were cast not as conscious political and moral choices but as psychic aberrations, proof that the right-wing voter, no matter how rational his choices or behaviour, was actually a would be dictator possessed of an inherently diseased mind. Those who today continually liken Trump to Hitler, or who ignore the history of left-wing atrocities, or who think all traditionalists are fascists, or who demonise rational objections to Islam as 'Islamophobia' are therefore repeating tropes established by Adorno and his colleagues in 1950. By 1954, Nathan Glazer was noting how this book had shaped the direction of research in all universities. Academics would spend decades looking for ways to illustrate that right-wing thinking was a kind of pathology. By our own time, such a view would be a fundamental political assumption on the part of nearly every academic.

Fundamental flaws in the research methodology of The Authoritarian Personality still dominate academia today. Think of the way in which Cultural Marxists, when speaking of the horrors of imperialism or conquest or war, only seem aware of Western examples of these. Think of the way in which the relatively benign British Empire (undoubtedly one of, if not the least deliberately evil empires in history) is critiqued, but we are given the impression that Imperial Japan was not conducting vile medical experiments or slaughtering the Chinese. Consider the way in which the Mongolian or Ottoman Empires, if the notable silence of Cultural Marxists is to be believed, swept through Europe and Asia with a childlike innocence and a firm commitment to female rights. In the Authoritarian Personality, the research consisted almost entirely of questioning white middle class Americans. Lo and behold, authoritarianism was discovered to be mainly a white problem, something which the US and the UK, or at a push Europe, might see more of than Africa, Asia or South America (the exact reverse of history as a whole).

There is, however, another racial issue that should be mentioned in connection with the Frankfurt School, and this indeed is one that concerns right-wing politics. There are white supremacists and white racists, and these individuals often cite the Frankfurt School as 'proof' of Jewish evil, of a Jewish plot to destroy the Western world. This is because many of the founders of the Frankfurt School and leading academics within it were Jewish. It should be noted that I totally detest and abhor that thinking, just as I detest Cultural Marxism. What anti-Semitism says about Jews is precisely what Cultural Marxism says about white people. There is no place in my critique of Cultural Marxism for that reductive, race-based stupidity. The race of any individual Cultural Marxist does not matter. It is the ideas that are toxic, not the ethnicity of their proponents.

I hope this book illustrates to at least some degree how we should never accept the racial tropes beloved by divisive Cultural Marxism. Those who follow sane, rational ideas generally prosper and create societies that flourish. Western civilisation flourished in the past by being right, by being right on the key economic and cultural drivers of success. It did not flourish by being mainly white, nor has it anything to be ashamed of in still being mainly white. And just as Jews denying Western values had a negative impact on academia, so too have Jews embodying Western values created the remarkable and worthy and embattled nation of Israel, from nothing. One of the worst features of Cultural Marxism is its refusal to view people as individuals rather than as racial types immediately slotted into "oppressor" and "victim" roles. We can hardly fight against it if we do the same thing.

21

THE COUNTER-CULTURE OF THE 1960S

"He and his cult survived on the generosity of hosts throughout California, and they were welcomed by most due to the counter-cultural practices of free love and communal living. The culminating murders were thus perpetrated due to Manson's strong ability to influence others, but the counter-culture provided for him an environment in which to cultivate and apply his psychopathy. Had he not been situated in the 1960s counter-culture, Manson would never have been able to exert control over and eventually commit murder through the members of the Manson Family."

—Robin Altman, *Sympathy for the Devil: Charles Manson's Exploitation of California's 1960s Counter-Culture*

IN THE BIG BROTHER SOCIETY OF *1984*, THE MOST dangerous and fanatical ideologues are all children. Adults like Citizen Smith do not just fear the party apparatus in power, they fear their own children and the children of their neighbours. Citizen Smith is more terrified of encounters with his neighbour's children than he is by encounters with officials of the all-encompassing State, even though he is well aware that the State has the power to arbitrarily arrest him, kill him and even erase his name from history.

What is it about children that makes them the perfect ideologues, and that ensures that they are more feared than the State they unthinkingly serve? It is surely the same realisation which informs William Golding's Lord of the Flies (written in 1954, exactly thirty years before the world depicted in 1984 but five years after the publication of Orwell's dystopian novel). A child's consciousness is more malleable than that of an adult, more susceptible to deliberate manipulation, but also more terrifyingly absolute when fixed by a barely understood political ideology on a path of power and oppression.

Child soldiers, whether in third-world conflicts, in fictional narratives, or recruited by drug gangs in modern cities, are symbolic of the absolute breakdown of social order, peace and normality, and of a brutality that can and will reach every member of that collapsing world. For these ideological killers to exist, adults must already have betrayed their children, and poisoned them with thoughts and beliefs no loving parent would share. But this betrayal is soon returned, as the lesson is learned too well and child fanatics become the most brutal members of their ideological group. To earn their place among adults, they will commit any atrocity. We see this today in the 'initiation' tasks older gang members set for 'youngers' in urban street culture, and the need of these children to earn 'respect' by doing that which should provoke horror.

Much sociological study has discussed the perverse inversion of family ties in such multigenerational criminal groups, where the gang becomes a substitute family and the willingness to inflict violence becomes a sign of 'adoption', 'brotherhood' or 'love'. Far less comment has passed, of course, on the way that Cultural Marxist assaults on traditional models of family life have actually prepared the ground for the kinds of society in which these twisted relationships flourish. Traditional family breakdown is the fertile soil upon which the seeds of gang culture spread, but as Orwell and Golding both knew, it is also the perfect environment in which totalitarian political systems can grow, untrammelled by more natural loyalties. Whether

Hitler Youth or Soviet Komsomol or Chinese Red Guard, youth has been consistently recruited by autocrats and tyrants, and has consistently provided these exploiters with their most fanatical followers.

It might of course be considered unjustified to link 'child' and 'youth' in this fashion as if there were no distinction between the two. A 'youth' in their late teens, such as the student revolutionaries of Mao's Red Guard or the student SJWs (social justice warriors) we see on US and UK campuses today, is different from a child of six, nine or twelve. But this is to ignore the sociological development that has passed in recent centuries or that marks the boundary between traditional and contemporary societies. In earlier times, lifespans were shorter and maturity developed sooner. A person who assumes a responsible adult role at fourteen, sixteen or eighteen becomes more mature than a person living an extended childhood by means of the absence of such responsibilities at twenty, twenty-five or thirty.

Social changes as the result of supposedly benevolent policies have deferred effective adulthood in Western civilisation. Welfare societies and growing university attendance have effectively extended responsibility-free childhood, with a concomitant growth in the popularity of immature, simplistic, adolescent or dangerous political solutions. A person of eighteen with a home, a wife and a child which they must support by their own efforts is busy doing just that (as the traditional working class often still are), whereas a State-funded perpetual student has both the leisure and the inclination to experiment with already failed ideologies (as well as easy access to them and the kind of adults — who may be intelligent but remarkably childlike in their own political development — happy to spread them).

This is one of the reasons why middle-class students are actually more susceptible to Cultural Marxism or other forms of anti-Western extremism (like Islamism on campus) than working-class individuals who are engaged in full-time employment. We see the truth of this in Britain today, with the willingness of university-educated perpetual children to interpret the

anti-capitalist, anti-Semitic, pro-terrorist and economically illiterate prejudices of Corbynism as the embodiment of hope. A sort of 'Poundshop' cult
of personality focused on a near-octogenarian MP with no oratorical ability
or intellectual credibility to explain that devotion is solely a consequence,
not of Corbyn's innate appeal, but of the adolescent inability to reason and
evaluate maturely which is actually encouraged at modern institutions of
'learning'.

Students learn dogma by rote in universities today, rather than the genuine critical skills of the Western intellectual tradition. This perfectly equips
them to accede to and mindlessly propagate whatever received opinions
academic Cultural Marxists wish to impart. As with other Cultural Marxists,
an inverse value system applies, where the degree to which they refuse to
think for themselves is validated as 'intelligence' and the degree to which they
avoid or disdain key contradictory texts is described as 'education'. Academic
achievement is therefore a measure of conformity rather than intellect.

Perhaps the purest expression of the chilling capacity of ideologically
driven youth to enact barbarisms at which many adults would baulk can be
seen during Mao's Cultural Revolution of the 1960s (thus far, thankfully, our
Corbynistas primarily concentrate on excusing and supporting historical
atrocities rather than repeating them. It could be, of course, that they are
working up the courage). The whole sorry and predictable Communist litany
of mob violence, show trials, internal purges, forced famine, economic insanity, sudden arrests, lynchings, shootings, beatings, tortures and executions
occurred at Mao's direction through both the ironically named 'Great Leap
Forward' and the Cultural Revolution that followed.

The youth of the Red Guard were enthusiastically involved in the most
brutal moments of this foul, pathetic saga. Mao delighted in their loyalty and
praised their devotion, a devotion he had anticipated in *The Little Red Book*.
This text acted as a constant guide for the Red Guard, especially its praise
of youth and encouragement to youth that they should dictate the nature

of the society everyone else inhabited. "The world is yours" Mao intoned, "You young people, full of vigour and vitality, are in the bloom of life…The world belongs to you. China's future belongs to you." And armed with this sense of ownership, youth proceeded to happily, joyously, with much vigour and vitality, beat Mao's enemies to death.

Of course, it is no more directly true to compare The Red Guard and Corbynistas today than it is for Cultural Marxists to accuse Trump of being Hitler. We must note that there has been no Great Leap Forward, no mass famines, no State-backed executions in a West troubled by Cultural Marxist youth. Yet, surely fear of Cultural Marxist youth is actually more justified and that youth more likely to lead to tyranny than the often mythical spectre of right-wing totalitarianism, which has been in justified disgrace ever since WWII. A youth who defines himself as a Nazi will most definitely be excluded, ostracised and ridiculed (as he or she should be, if the label is true). A youth who wears a Che Guevara t-shirt and calls himself a Communist is not subject to the same opprobrium. A 'respectable' academic can dominate the field of history and have his views inform school textbooks both before and after stating that Communist mass murders were justified, as Hobsbawn did. An academic with a similarly bizarre or morally obscene attitude to Nazism will not remain in a post, let alone be respected.

This free pass for Communism holds sway in wider society outside the narrow corridors of the university. Self-professed Communists are invited onto debate programmes to represent the voice of youth, with no recognition of the central irony that there is nothing either rebellious or youthful about being wedded to an extremist ideology that is over a century old and that has created death camps and destroyed freedom and lives wherever it has been attempted. Would a self-declared young Nazi be asked on daytime television for their views on Brexit, for example? Hardly, unless it were solely with the intention of smearing all supporters of Brexit.

Nor should we ignore the fact that senior current Labour Party figures have advocated the same tactics that were enacted by the Red Guard. John McDonnell, the Shadow Chancellor, has joked about kneecapping political opponents. He has called for every single Tory to be hounded and harassed in public. He has directly praised terrorism, stating that the bombs and bullets of the IRA secured peace. This is not only sharing their aims for Irish reunification, it should be noted, but praising their terrorist methods. Owen Jones, the Guardian journalist, did the same. McDonnell found it amusing to respond to criticism of his history of supporting extremism by waving a copy of *The Little Red Book* in Parliament. After the Grenfell fire, he called for public insurrection — for actual, presumably violent, uprising. Diane Abbott, Shadow Home Secretary, stated in a television appearance that Mao (the greatest mass murderer in human history) did 'more good than bad'. Corbyn himself has called Hamas (the child-murdering terrorist group Hamas, not some lovable alternative that unfortunately shares the same name) his friends.

The current Labour leadership have all spent 30 years or more sharing platforms with terrorist murderers, bombers and leaders, delivering eulogies and laying wreaths at their graves, justifying both their aims and their actions, socialising and befriending enemies of the West who have blood on their hands. And these same people are now leading one of the two main parties of our supposed liberal and moderate democracy, are now at the very heart of our political establishment, and are now supported by millions of people who paradoxically consider themselves democrats opposed to tyranny. These same people are free to opine that, say, Brexit voters or Trump supporters are fascists, whilst having a history far in excess of that of any Brexiteer or Trump voter, of actually supporting political violence. Their own extremism is, of course, dismissed as mere smears by their fanatical, often perpetually adolescent, admirers.

How do these things relate either to Cultural Marxism or the heading of this section of the book, the Counter-Cultural Revolution of the 1960s? They relate because the current leadership of the Labour Party are elderly perpetual children, united with their youthful followers by a refusal to ever grow up or ever develop an adult understanding of the world and a mature and objective view of Western civilisation. For just as Mao was using youth for his bloody Chinese reign of terror, Western civilisation itself experienced a cultural revolution which whilst less immediately bloody has perhaps had longer-term effects and is still causing damage today. With the fictional warnings of Orwell and Golding and Huxley ignored, Western civilisation undertook the complete prioritisation of the ignorance and totalitarianism of youth in the political sphere.

France, so often the crucible of ideas (especially dangerous ones), indulged in a sort of limited, recreationally destructive repeat of the French Revolution in the student uprisings of 1968. British politicians in the same decade found for the first time that youthful pop stars, comics and DJs were far more socially influential than themselves, whilst some scrambled to adopt and implement 'progressive' policies designed to undermine the family, traditional virtues and adult responsibilities as thoroughly as possible. In the US, the hippie movement and anti-Vietnam protests tapped a deep and apparently inexhaustible wellspring of youthful certainty, like an oil well pumping out a black fluid of combustible ideas. At the most toxic edges, this movement adopted the certainty that any crime they committed was a necessary form of self-expression. Peace, love and rejection of 'the Man' became John Lennon funding the IRA or Charles Manson's 'wives' torturing Sharon Tate to death.

Individualism in its most selfish expressions was therefore a consequence of this seismic cultural shift towards the political power of youth. Like the proto-anarchism of Diogenes, self-expression, a kind of social and political vanity, took the place of self-development. Youth saw itself in the mirror of society, and fell in love with its own image. Politics became narcissism, which still informs the virtue signalling of all Cultural Marxist positions. Older Cultural Marxists encouraged this shift in the same way that older gang leaders recruit young drug couriers and footsoldiers, as tools to allow and spread their own power. Just as the high ideals of the French Revolution or the *Little Red Book's* praise of youth led to violent mob barbarities, so too did the prioritisation of youth recruit to the Cultural Marxist cause gullible individuals who could easily be swayed by the weakest of emotional arguments. We see this in both the 1960s hippie generation and the current Millennial generation (sadly the most deluded and self-indulgent generation since the baby boomers and hippies of the 1960s). Today, the people who were young fools hating Western civilisation in the late 1960s and early 1970s are the respected elder statesmen of the parties admired by Millennials. They shaped succeeding generations in their own flawed image.

The prioritisation of adolescent thinking within politics since the counter-culture of the 1960s has had a profound impact on the choices made by Western nations ever since. Youth has been deified to the extent that today we see adults in their thirties, forties or even their sixties thinking and behaving, or trying to think and behave, like teenagers. The middle-aged man who dresses like a twenty-year-old and the death of the sober fashions of maturity which were once commonplace (the suits, hats, pipes and umbrellas) is only the most trivial outward manifestation of a radical and ultimately political shift of power between generations. As power has shifted, so has the nature of rebellion itself, growing once again more immediate and violent as the recklessness of youth dominates the mature reflection of adulthood.

The actual rebels today, then, in terms of cultural attitudes, are those who cling to any traditional conception of generational roles, particularly the idea that any automatic authority accrues to one's elders. Student activism is no longer a fringe of politics, but a central battleground dominated by the flags of the Left. We see this in the invitations extended to bloggers and opinionated children to share the benefit of their limited experience in television debates or commentaries, and in the way in which the natural realisation that youth might make these experiences more limited or less valid as general principles is now the thing that would shock, rather than the spectacle of mature adults grimly mimicking the attitudes of people who have never held any real responsibility.

Society is, however, robbed of both wisdom and experience in decision-making when nobody acknowledges that the view of a sixty-year-old may indeed be better formed (and informed) than that of a fifteen-year-old. Indeed, we see again an exact reversal of traditional values thanks to Cultural Marxism. Where once the benevolence of a civilisation was judged by the manner in which it treated its elderly and infirm, today we see loud calls for the votes of the elderly to be ignored and widespread contempt for any attitudes to issues like mass immigration they might possess based on actual experience. Combined with the deliberate distortion of the historical record, the prioritisation of youth allows Cultural Marxists to circumvent those who might actually know and have lived factual realities, contrary to their own ideologically driven fictions regarding the past.

22

FEMINISM

"The people that hold that our culture is an oppressive patriarchy, they don't want to admit that the current hierarchy might be predicated on competence."

—Jordan Peterson

THE PROPOSITION THAT MEN AND WOMEN HAVE equal rights and are deserving of an equal dignity and respect within society is not one that many people in Western nations would dispute, certainly not if they are themselves of Western origin. But it is only a century since the vote was conferred on women, and only really in the world post-WWI that the ability to pursue a career in almost any field has been open to women as a whole. While powerful women are extremely common in the history of the West dating back to its very origins, there is no doubt that the status and opportunities they possess today exceed those open to them for most of the past. The process of acquiring an equality of rights is in and of itself a natural and noble thing, and it is the desire for liberty and the pursuit of happiness shared by both men and women of all classes, cultures and nations.

The feminist movement, then, begins with an assumption that few would dispute: that society itself and individual lives within it are improved by recognising a political and professional equality between the genders. Like many other broad attitudes within the framework of Cultural Marxism, there is a deceptive justice to the initial proposition which is soon contradicted by subsequent demands. For what we see with feminism today, just as with Cultural Marxist attitudes to race, is an initially noble intention soon perverted into a series of ignoble prejudices. Contemporary feminism no longer seeks to redress a social structure that prioritises males. That battle, if feminists and society itself were prepared to be honest on this topic, was won some time ago as far as Western civilisation is concerned.

The cultures today in which the rights of women are not championed, and in which women are by birth gender assigned a subordinate role in society, are not those of Western nations or of Western civilisation as a whole. Yet the vast majority of feminists have nothing to say regarding these real oppressions by gender. A rare feminist with the moral courage to confront the misogyny of Islamic culture, Anne-Marie Waters, was effectively forced out of a 'mainstream' British party, not once, but twice. In spotting this silence regarding non-Western cultures and volubility regarding the most female-friendly societies on Earth, we can discern other flaws in the product feminism offers. Feminism today does not seek the redress of wrongs but the imposition of fresh injustices. It aims not for the emancipation of women but for the disenfranchisement of men. It does not challenge stereotypes and fight discrimination, but rather spreads stereotypes and requires discrimination which is unjust towards all those who happen to have been born with male genitalia.

We do not need to look far within feminism itself to find proof of these assertions, for self-declared feminists (particularly academic leaders of the movement) themselves make it very clear in repeated statements that the nature of their project is not about equality or justice in any meaningful sense. Such an intention would require a desire for injustices towards women to cease, rather than a desire for injustices towards men to be inflicted. But it is notable today how much of feminist rhetoric has become a quite chilling and completely open expression of hatred. Just a few examples from the decades of bile pumped out by radical feminism for more than thirty years now should suffice to make the point:

"I want to see a man beaten to a bloody pulp with a high-heel shoved in his mouth, like an apple in the mouth of a pig." Andrea Dworkin.

"The proportion of men must be reduced and maintained at approximately 10% of the human race." Sally Miller Gearhart.

"I do want to be able to explain to a 9-year-old boy in terms he will understand why I think it's OK for girls to wear shirts that revel in their superiority over boys." Treena Shapiro.

"I feel that 'man-hating' is an honorable and viable political act." Robin Morgan.

"All men are rapists and that's all they are." Marilyn French.

In just these few examples, we see the open acknowledgement that the ideology being expressed is about hatred and loathing of another group. We see the assumption that all males are somehow a monolithic block, who think and feel and act in exactly the same way, and that this block requires destruction. We see a casual, flippant belief expressed in the necessity of some kind of vast social change that would require in the first instance hundreds of millions of murders and in the second instance some ongoing programme of abortions or infant murders to maintain an arbitrarily selected demographic percentage.

Other feminist statements that can be found within seconds of any internet search include women stating that they would terminate any male baby, that all men are rapists, that men are mere walking dildos, that men are less than animals, that men are responsible for all evil in human history, that any entirely female society would be harmonious and peaceful (such feminists take little account of actual female interactions that contradict this notion), that male words, looks, gestures, seating postures (essentially everything men do no matter how harmless) are acts of violent assault, that men should be castrated, gassed or otherwise eliminated, that men are incapable of real love, compassion, or affection of any kind, or that all men are engaged in a perpetual conspiracy against women (I've never received the memo, personally, or the secret hand signals, or the membership card).

Confronted with extremism of this kind, there are only really two natural reactions. The first is to see those expressing these ideas as comical figures, rendered pathetic by the depths of their own hatred and the patent absurdity of their declarations. And it *is* easy to laugh at these kinds of statements. The second reaction, however, comes with further thought, and that is a reaction of horror. For what exactly would happen if any one of those people who thought this way, instead of being vitriolic journalists, academics, teachers of gender studies classes, placard-waving loons at fringe protest meetings, directors of feminist cinema, obscure playwrights or angry musicians, were actually in political power? What would happen to a society in which hating half of the populace purely on the basis of their gender was entirely normal and the political system acted on this hate?

What would happen, at first, might be very similar to what happens today. The gender which is subject to this loathing would find itself deliberately and legally excluded from employment opportunities. It would find that it was perfectly legal for a company to promote someone else ahead of them on the basis of gender. They would find that positions could be advertised as only requiring female candidates. They would find that all-female shortlists had been put in place. They would find that major advertisers hired feminist directors to present hate-filled pieces, of little relevance to the product being sold, which characterised their gender as monstrous (as Gillette have done recently). They would find that it became normal for people to dismiss their arguments, not on the basis of any logical refutation of the points made, but just because these points were made by a man. They would find that a whole array of ceremonies, speeches, awards, talking points, interviews, films, books, songs and paintings expressed an endless variation on the same essential theme of the inherent worthlessness of their gender, and that, increasingly, any manifestation of a statement of contempt towards their gender was treated as somehow brave, worthy or laudable and the person making it as a good example to others.

And this would only be the beginning of the hate they discovered. They would find that an entire academic discipline and millions of hours of lectures and classes had been paid for and conducted, all essentially repeating the same idea that everything about men deserves contempt. They would find the word 'toxic' appended to their gender, as if its inherently poisonous nature were beyond question. All these things already take place.

Of course, to some the idea of lamenting or fearing these developments, or even of considering them deeply unjust, will itself be ludicrous, but those that do respond that way are sure to have been conditioned to such a dismissive response by feminism itself, or by general Cultural Marxist attitudes. It could also be pointed out that there are degrees of feminism, as with all political movements, and that perhaps the hate-filled comments quoted above and ones similar to them represent an extreme of feminist thinking not shared by the vast bulk of other feminists. To an extent, such a criticism would be true, but it should be remembered that my point in discussing all of these Cultural Marxist developments is to highlight the ways in which they are dangerous.

I do not therefore have an issue with those who simply wish to help women or promote fairness and decency towards women. Indeed, part of my point is that this idea of justice has already been, for quite some time, a cultural norm within our society. It is the transition from that understanding of equality towards a new imposition of inequality that I seek to highlight and warn against. There is very little point in any social advance if it merely reverses the roles of who suffers and who prospers. It is only an objective improvement of society if suffering is removed, rather than transferred.

A milder feminist might assert that while they do not hate men it is clear that society is still structured to favour men. The arguments usually placed to support this concern the gender pay gap, the supposed glass ceiling, and the greater than demographically consistent representation of men in positions of power within our society. But the very fact that these arguments are still made ironically contradicts the idea they express. Because the plain truth is that these arguments were logically and convincingly refuted nearly forty years ago. Thomas Sowell provided lengthy and eloquent rebuttals of these ideas, backed by evidence, throughout the 1970s.

Sowell noted that whilst a disparity between average pay levels did exist between men and women, there were specific reasons for this that had nothing to do with any conspiratorial prioritisation of men within society. Women were on average paid less than men because more women took lengthy career breaks or accepted part-time positions of employment. It takes time to establish the best careers, and men were investing more time in their careers. Higher pay by comparison with women therefore only reflects a greater length of service and consequently a greater opportunity to reach the higher positions. This was true in the 1970s. This is still true today.

The gender pay gap has in fact narrowed but not because women were unjustly treated and now are slightly less unjustly treated. It has primarily narrowed because women are having fewer children, having children later in life, and returning to full-time employment more quickly than they once did. Female choices, to have a child and give up a career or have a child and return to a career quickly or not have children at all, moderate female pay far more than any imaginary conspiracy by men, unless one supposes that every woman who has a career break is forced to do so by some overbearing partner. Biology explains the pay gap, not oppression.

Given Sowell's work, since confirmed by others, which shows that the gender pay gap is largely illusory (Sowell offered similar logical rebuttals of racial wealth gaps as proof of discrimination), one might ask why, if our society is so predisposed towards men, the work of this particular male has been so consistently ignored, whilst the far more subjective 'feeling' of inequality advocated by feminists is still widely endorsed? Would not a society structured to favour men have leapt on Sowell's reasoned arguments and stopped assuming that women were subject to employment injustices that didn't actually exist? But our society did not do that. Instead, it busily set about addressing the illusory injustice with further legislation that discriminated against men. And it is still doing so, forty years after the idea behind that legislation was debunked. We have actually found that if any structural bias based on gender exists, it is against men, for logical, rational arguments placed by men are automatically trumped by subjective, anecdotal and emotional arguments placed by women.

If we look beyond the gender pay gap and reference more recent developments with regard to critiques of feminism, we see the same process — of society still acting on feminist ideas that have been thoroughly and accurately refuted. One of the most famous Jordan Peterson interviews illustrates this point. Peterson was told by a feminist interviewer that society favoured men. That view was self-evident because most CEOs of major companies are male, most leading politicians are still male, and most of the highest remunerated jobs in society are still primarily occupied by males. This is essentially the pyramid argument of gender discrimination: men are at the top, so women must be at the bottom. It is, of course, a logical fallacy, because it depends on exactly how much of the pyramid we are shown.

Peterson more eloquently refuted the pyramid idea when he pointed out that taking the achievements of a tiny, tiny fraction of men, the most financially successful elite, and extrapolating from that to consider their experience pertinent to all male experience is absurd. The homeless, unemployed male does not gain any benefit from the maleness he shares with the CEO. He will not have access to becoming a CEO purely by dint of maleness, nor will the male CEO act with special regard or solicitation towards the homeless male because they both have male genitalia. Peterson then listed the ways in which male experience is more negative than female experience (higher suicide rates, higher workplace mortality, higher stress and depression rates, earlier mortality, higher rates of homelessness, higher rates of violent death, higher rates of alcohol and drug dependency, etc.), asking: if society privileges men, where exactly is this privilege in these areas?

Elsewhere, Peterson has pointed out the role played by male and female psychological characteristics, for which a wealth of evidence — some contributed by Peterson himself — exists and regarding which he is an acknowledged authority. Whilst it has become an uncomfortable thing to acknowledge in our society, there are chemical, hormonal and biological differences between men and women, some of which might lend themselves to greater success in certain occupations. Males are biologically on average stronger and faster than women, and this has an effect on sports performance or physical jobs, for example. More than this, there are mental characteristics which, on average, are found more frequently in either the male or female brain, owing to differences of brain structure and chemistry. These may also play a part in causing variations in performance within different occupations, or predispose genders towards different occupations. Nature, rather than conspiracy, may explain some disparities of attainment.

Cultural Marxism, of course, is uncomfortable with any biological facts which render its own narratives of victimhood redundant, and so Peterson's public use of such facts has been recast as 'misogyny' or 'prejudice' or 'far-right thinking', in line with the standard smears deployed against any challenge to the supremacy of Cultural Marxist attitudes. Indeed, where Sowell's work was ignored, Peterson's is actively traduced, purely because his objective analysis contradicts the subjective fictions on which Cultural Marxism and its components, such as feminism, entirely rely.

Sadly, we cannot even say that leading feminists have restricted themselves to hypocritically hate-filled language or the denial of basic biological facts. Some have applied the logic of their ideology in action. When the Women's March movement began, it might have been easy to dismiss it as a virtue-signalling display of Cultural Marxist righteousness and leave it at that. The absurdity of the 'pussy hat' as a form of protest (from people triggered by the MAGA hat when worn by Trump supporters) and the incoherent nature of the protests themselves, unsure of whether they objected to the word pussy in a ten year old private conversation, totally unproven allegations of sexual abuse, equally unproven accusations of racism or just the fact that the country had elected an old white male after a younger black male, spoke for themselves. But one of the leading instigators and organisers of the Washington Women's March against Trump, Donna Hylton, personally represented the kind of moral self-blindness the extremes of feminism engage in. I have previously referenced this case but will give a fuller description of it here because it is very instructive.

Hylton came to prominence as an ex-convict feminist, an advocate of 'women's rights' and prison reform. What was not discussed in most of the mainstream press was the nature of Hylton's conviction and the connection between it and her supposedly noble feminist credentials. She had been convicted of second-degree murder and two counts of first-degree kidnapping after being part of a seven-woman gang who had plotted and carried out the abduction and murder of Long Island real estate broker Thomas Vigliarole. Their victim was tempted with the prospect of sex after three of the group posed as prostitutes to lure him to a Harlem apartment that had been prepared for his murder. Over the course of 15-20 days of obscene violence, Vigliarole was drugged, repeatedly beaten, starved, burned and tortured by methods including the forceful insertion of a three-foot long steel rod into his anus and squeezing the victim's testicles with a pair of pliers. Neither Hylton nor any of the other torturers showed any remorse for the murder and detectives who interviewed her commented on her emotionless, cold-blooded responses.

Hylton was not only an organiser but also a featured speaker on the Woman's March. Her brutal murderous past was not, according to thousands of righteous feminists, any question mark over her character or her suitability for a leadership role within their movement. At the same time as listening to the pious declarations of a convicted torture killer, feminists saw fit to cast themselves as moral guardians of the nation outraged by Trump's behaviour. The word 'pussy', or male locker room chat about the availability of willing sexual partners if you happen to be a billionaire, was considered by these feminists as worse than the rape and murder of a man by psychopathically violent women. A large portion of society, in neither caring to examine the few commentaries that criticised Hylton's involvement or condemn her self-election as a moral authority, agreed. The United States as a society, thanks to feminism, seemed to be declaring that rude or boorish talk by men was worse than savage torture and homicide by women.

It is not only on the grounds of propagating hatred towards men or enacting violence towards them that contemporary feminism has strayed far beyond any justifiable intent. Not satisfied with steering society towards legal discrimination against males or with making violent pronouncements about millions of entirely innocent males, feminists have sought to take a leading role in poisoning interactions between races and have sought to demonise white people just as they demonise anyone who happens to be male. The most vile racial theory widely extant and officially condoned in the West today is that of white privilege, and this absurd fiction, by which each and every white person on the planet is deemed to benefit from automatic advantages at the expense of others, was a theory first fully expounded by feminist academics (although it drew on earlier commentaries by black intellectuals).

The first full description of white privilege came in an article called 'White Privilege: Unpacking the Invisible Knapsack', written by feminist academic Peggy McIntosh in 1988 and first published in the ironically titled 'Peace and

'Freedom' magazine in 1989. Just like the structuralists and post-structuralists, McIntosh was interested in detecting invisible systems of power, explaining how they operate and proposing how a fairer and better society could avoid their influence. The trouble, of course, with the detection of invisible objects is that they may be invisible because they don't exist or are purely figments of the delusional imagination of the one person who magically discerns something which nobody before them was capable of detecting.

McIntosh's article is fascinating both for the huge influence it has had on subsequent Cultural Marxists and on social attitudes generally. It marks the point at which entire branches of academia abandoned any remaining vestige of respect towards the intellectual heritage of the West and the established traditions of logic and reason by which scholarly enquiry had previously functioned. The structuralists had claimed that the walls of Western thought were less important than the mortar that held them together, the post-structuralists had claimed that the wall and the mortar were illusory, but it was articles like McIntosh's that smashed the wall down and salted the ground like victorious Romans after the fall of Carthage. McIntosh's article is an example of the triumph of philistine barbarism in the very institutions that should be a bulwark against it.

The argument McIntosh advances, such as it is, asserts that all white people are privileged and unaware of that privilege. In a circular manner repeated by other believers in this nonsense ever since, any denial of the invisible privilege is further proof of its existence (a similar logic is deployed by those with serious psychological conditions. Oliver Sacks, for example, describes a condition that causes those who possess it to insist that they are dead. When it is pointed out to them that they have a heartbeat, they reply that obviously dead people can have a heartbeat because they are dead and possess one). The 'evidence' that McIntosh provides for this comes in the form of an extended confession, with the word 'I' recurring multiple times in a list of purely subjective claims. McIntosh tells us, for example, that she can 'arrange to be in the company of people of my race most of the time'. Her idea is that black people or other ethnic minorities cannot do this. The fact that this hugely sweeping generalisation is contradicted by almost all ethnic minority experience in the West (where many ethnic groups live in self-forming segregation) does not register, nor does the idea that in many parts of the world, the numbers of white people, and their ability to cohere in social groups of their choosing, is far more limited than that of non-whites in the West.

Somehow, then, an experience that is not general, that when it occurs is more likely caused by probability related to numbers available rather than active oppression, is given as one of a series of 'proofs' of sustained, systemic, conspiratorial oppression and active, perpetual, malicious privilege. A total of 26 similarly absurd general statements of supposed privilege follow, each backed not by statistical evidence, logical enquiry or rational thought, but by subjective emotional feeling. Each one is felt to be true, and therefore true. Each one is an anecdote, a purely personal 'experience' reconstituted as an axiomatic social reality. It is the kind of evidence that only a lunatic ideologue would consider as evidence.

At the same time as generalising all white and all black experience through the lens of their subjective feeling, McIntosh and other proponents of white privilege believe that no white person can ever understand the experience of any non-white person. Human empathy or sympathy cannot bridge that gap, apparently, but the white Cultural Marxist simultaneously acquires the right to speak on behalf of those she cannot, by dint of her own skin colour, ever understand. She can speak of both black and white experience, both male and female experience, with complete authority, whilst explaining to us that no white man can achieve the same. McIntosh can speak for the universal human condition, but Shakespeare cannot. After all, Shakespeare was neither a feminist, nor black, nor even a white feminist of the mid-twentieth century, endowed by ideology alone with the capacity to pronounce final judgement on whole genders and races.

It is truly astonishing just how far McIntosh departs, not only from what was once thought of as required academic rigour but from rationality itself. Her essay is a howl more than an argument, the exact opposite of reasoned enquiry, an evidence-free list of subjective assertions and hypocritical prejudice. And this has formed the basis of what passes for much academic 'scholarship' ever since. The contribution of feminism to Cultural Marxism has been the prioritisation of hysterical emoting over logical thought and the normalisation of a racist hate theory as a mainstream component of contemporary attitudes.

We should finally note a recent development that represents the absolute moral sewer, by any traditional or objective standards, feminism has become. In New York, a law has been passed that allows abortion beyond 24 weeks, up to and including full term, moments before birth. When questioned on the law, one of the proposers admitted that, if passed, terminations could occur when the mother is dilating and about to give birth. Full-term infants, capable of all the experience and consciousness of a delivered baby, can be murdered, quite legally, under this legislation. A supposedly civilised modern nation has legally endorsed infanticide.

Defenders of the legislation note that such terminations can only take place with the agreement of the attending physician, and in cases where the life or health of the mother is at issue. But they do not note that fifty years of prior abortion legislation and case history has established that 'health' does not refer solely to life-threatening conditions for either the mother or the child. It can include a whole range of psychological, religious, contextual or even economic justifications, indeed anything that the mother *thinks* is pertinent to her health, *thinks* is more significant than the life of her child, and with which the professional being paid to conduct this termination agrees.

Essentially, therefore, it allows the mother and physician to make a subjective value call, on the basis of which a life is terminated. Feminism has now become so perverse that the feelings of a mother, however transitory or unjustified, can be valued as superior to the life of her child. It is her right to kill that exceeds the right of the child to live. This is, of course, the exact opposite of every moral lesson which a healthy and rational society imparts to mothers under any circumstance.

23

The Nature of the Beast: What We Are Fighting Against

"….we can endure neither our vices nor the
remedies needed to cure them."

—Livy, *The History of Rome, Books 1-5:*
The Early History of Rome

The purpose of this book is twofold. It is intended, firstly, to offer a relatively simple and accurate summary of what Western civilisation is, without getting too theoretical or too distracted by competing claims. One cannot defend or recognise the worth of something which one does not understand or have a clear image of. The secondary purpose is to present a similarly limited but exact definition of Cultural Marxism. One cannot defeat an enemy without knowing the nature of that enemy. The entire book is therefore an exercise in definition, as perhaps any extended intellectual effort becomes.

So let us define Cultural Marxism, more fully than we have before. Cultural Marxism is one of the two existential threats Western civilisation faces today. Make no mistake, if Cultural Marxism achieves its objectives, Western civilisation ceases to exist, and is replaced with a far more tyrannical and absolutist alternative. Untold damage has already been done to the security, the unity and the harmony of the West by Cultural Marxists in positions of power and influence. Millions of people opposed to Western civilisation, its achievements, its history and the continuation of its values, have been trained to despise the West in Western universities or via Cultural-Marxist-controlled news sources and entertainment sources. Millions more fundamentally opposed to Western values and wedded to an alien ideology with distinctly antagonistic moral codes, primarily ones centred in Islamic teaching, have been invited intro Western nations. Increasingly, these two existential threats act in concert, supporting each other in ways that hasten Western decline.

Cultural Marxism is hatred of and opposition to Western civilisation. It is the history teacher or history curriculum that concentrates solely on Western crimes. It is the syllabus that devotes itself to Western practices of slavery and oppression in the 17th, 18th or 19th centuries, without noting the non-Western practice of that universal human crime before, during and since the West abandoned it. It is the stand-up routine that treats slavery and imperialism as if they are relevant and topical issues of the 21st century, whilst ignoring the crimes of Islam occurring today. It is the student communist with the Che t-shirt and the idiotically limited conception of history, influenced by his Marxist teachers. It is the Antifa thug with the masked face, deciding that classical liberals are Nazis.

And it is more than just individuals motivated by hypocritical hatreds. It is the hate legislation that prioritises the victimhood of certain special groups, and the ethnic or gender or sexual orientation pressure group that demands special treatment, additional employment, or further protection than that provided to any other citizen. It is the college lecturer who insists on the existence of an illusory 'patriarchy' or a purely mythical 'white privilege'. It is the hundreds of billions of pounds that has been set aside by affirmative action and similar discriminatory and redistributive programmes by governments and international agencies. It is the politician who encourages open borders and mass migration, who designates sanctuary cities in the US, or who seeks to imprison critics or silence criticism of mass immigration.

And in the age of the Internet, these absurdities spread swifter than the Black Death through medieval ports. The technological achievements of Western civilisation convey messages of hate about Western civilisation. For Cultural Marxism is the hypocritical bigot online whose only knowledge of British history is a pejorative reading of the Irish Potato Famine. It is the selectivity that notices only the measures that Israel takes to defend itself, and none of the terrorism which requires such measures in response, and then spews skewed commentary in the great vomitorium of Twitter. It is the funding of Palestinian, Afghan or Pakistani madrasas where children are taught to hate Westerners and Jews, such funding coordinated and given in the name of the populations targeted by that hate, applauded by official bodies in press releases.

Nor is its influence limited to the spheres of academia or politics. It is dominant in Hollywood and entertainment. It is the film director who portrays the IRA or Hamas as heroes, and the political party that does the same. It is the journalist, TV anchor or entire network that devotes itself exclusively to undermining Western nation states, Western traditional values and Western populations. It is the UN stocking human rights commissions and committees with representatives of the worst regimes on the planet, whilst sending other agents to criticise and smear nations like Britain, the US and Israel. It is every way in which the resources and the freedoms and the wealth of the West are diverted towards the destruction and the harm and the death of the West and all it stands for, quite deliberately. It is not a conspiracy directed by any single source, but a vast, shared, powerful network of aligned stupidities and hypocritical and socially damaging ideas together with the gullible, the wicked and the corrupt who adhere to these notions.

To summarise the points I have been making thus far or which are most important in defining Cultural Marxism, we must remember the following:

1. Cultural Marxism is hatred of Western civilisation. This includes hatred of Western culture, history, values, ethnic groups, religions and nation states.

2. Cultural Marxists tend to oppose and despise all of Western civilisation. Individuals can hate particular elements of Western civilisation without being Cultural Marxists. If they subscribe to a hatred of the entirety, they are Cultural Marxists.

3. Cultural Marxism is a largely middle-class movement, drawing its leaders from the middle and upper class. The working class tend to be inherently suspicious of Cultural Marxism.

4. Cultural Marxists despise the traditional working class, especially the white working class of nations like the US and UK. They will always act in ways contrary to the interests of this class.

5. Cultural Marxists nevertheless believe that they own the votes of the working class, often drawing upon historical connections they themselves have betrayed. They may offer corrupt forms of patronage to the working class, but use this solely as a means of controlling them and actually preventing the working class themselves attaining any real power or influencing policy.

6. Cultural Marxists only respect those who are also Cultural Marxists. All other groups are to be manipulated or destroyed.

7. Cultural Marxists impose no traditional moral judgements on their own actions or on the actions of other Cultural Marxists. They will only do so when forced to do so by public outcry.

8. Cultural Marxists define good and evil solely by reference to Cultural Marxism. Value judgements of individuals or policies will concentrate solely on how these individuals or policies advance Cultural Marxism.

9. Cultural Marxist morality will often directly reverse traditional moral judgements. Actions previously defined as evil will be defined as good, and vice versa. Victims will be defined as oppressors, and oppressors as victims.

10. Cultural Marxists will prize individual liberty wherever it represents self-indulgence or antisocial tendencies. They will oppose individual liberty wherever it questions Cultural Marxism or provides individuals with the means to do so.

11. Cultural Marxists believe in a rigid hierarchy of victimhood. This hierarchy is based on a highly selective reading of history and on historical injustices. All individuals and ideas will be judged by reference to this hierarchy.

12. The hierarchy of victimhood places ethnic minorities above white people, women above men, homosexuals above heterosexuals, illegal residents above legal citizens, foreign interests above national interests, the disabled above the able, and transsexuals or other minority groups above the most common groups. All of these categories must be enforced on others but can be suspended or ignored for Cultural Marxists themselves, provided that they consistently express devotion to the hierarchy of victimhood.

13. To all Cultural Marxists, words matter more than actions. One must constantly signal devotion to Cultural Marxist attitudes that one does not necessarily act upon. Someone who expresses the words of devotion more often is more highly valued than someone who acts on those words. Others must also be forced to repeat the words, whether or not they believe them (as in the attempts to force Jordan Peterson to use imaginary pronouns).

14. Feelings matter more than facts. All Cultural Marxist ideas are based on emotional responses and prioritise emotion over logic or reason. The degree to which an idea is felt is more important than the degree to which it is true (see the 'confessional' personal exegesis mode of

feminist and 'white studies' critical theory from *Unpacking the Invisible Knapsack* onwards. Note also that hate speech is hate speech as long as anyone says it is, according to the British police.).

15. All Cultural Marxists reject the concept of truth. All truths are relative and conditional. All are based on systems of power. This applies to everything except everything that Cultural Marxism considers true, which is irrefutably true.

16. Cultural Marxists almost always consider violence towards non-Cultural-Marxists justified or excusable (see Antifa, Momentum, BLM, Labour Party support for the IRA and Hamas etc).

17. Cultural Marxists do not understand or support democracy. They will only respect democracy when it gives them what they want. Whenever it doesn't, they will consider it undemocratic, without any reference to the meaning of democracy itself (see Remain arguments in favour of a 'People's Vote').

18. Cultural Marxists see language as a political tool for imposing their own beliefs, rather than as a medium by which a shared meaning is conveyed. The meaning of every word is fluid and only exists to support Cultural Marxism. An entirely opposite meaning can be advanced for the same word if that is politically expedient. This is in fact a favoured tactic, as in Cultural Marxist understandings of 'democracy', 'border', 'sovereignty', 'influence', 'extremist', 'truth', 'fact', 'dreamer', 'social justice', 'equality', 'diversity', etc. Cultural Marxists will often deploy sophistry because they do not consider any shared meaning sacred (see the Remain convolutions and dishonesties even with such a simple word as 'leave').

19. Cultural Marxism derives its self-mythology from the French Revolution. All Cultural Marxists see themselves as continuing a rational Enlightenment tradition, even and sometimes particularly when, they destroy the best parts of the Enlightenment heritage. Modern

Cultural Marxism shares the same hypocrisies and propensity to violence as the French Revolution.

20. Cultural Marxism has aligned itself with Islam. Cultural Marxists will defend Islam from any criticism and advance Islam in any way they can.

21. Cultural Marxists do not believe in free speech. Since speech is a political weapon, it must be controlled by Cultural Marxists.

22. Cultural Marxists gravitate towards State employment (in the same way that child abusers gravitate towards childcare). State positions of authority allow them to advance the Cultural Marxist agenda. They always believe in a large State with interventionist powers over thought and speech.

23. Cultural Marxist attitudes to gender, sex, sexuality, family and all intimate personal interactions are dictated by feminist academic theory. Cultural Marxists detest any traditional family model and always prioritise and promote alternatives.

24. Cultural Marxists are particularly dominant in academia. Most Cultural Marxist ideas and actions will begin in a university environment and spread from there. They will deploy academic funding, research, teaching and authority in exactly the same ways they deploy the resources of any institution they control, to advance Cultural Marxist power.

25. Cultural Marxists show a contempt for history. This is two-fold, as the Cultural Marxist will specifically hate Western history but also have a contempt for history as a discipline. They will not bother to learn anything that does not advance a Cultural Marxist reading of history. They will tend never to engage with primary sources, and they will never weigh events and individuals objectively or strive towards an objective reading. History, like language, does not convey a shared meaning. It is, like language, there as a political tool, a weapon to advance Cultural Marxist dogma and orthodoxy. This will all be particularly true of

Cultural Marxist historians, who will all be polemicists with a very selective knowledge of history.

24

CONTROL OF HISTORY

"To destroy a people you must first sever their roots."

—Alexander Solzhenitsyn

THERE ARE REPEATED TACTICS THAT THE
Cultural Marxists deploy in their war against Western civilisation. Unlike
many on the Right or in the political middle who have long ignored the
importance of these areas in shaping social attitudes, Cultural Marxists are
always aware of the importance of controlling the cultural narrative extant
within society. They do this by dominating media, entertainment and both
high and low culture and the institutions associated with these. The absolute dominance of Cultural Marxism in media and entertainment has been
deployed continuously and more obviously than ever before in relation to
both the election of Trump in the US and the Brexit referendum result in the
UK, primarily because both these events were the first significant reversals
of the Cultural Marxist agenda in the West since the 1960s (with the possible
exception of the Thatcher-Reagan years, although neither of these otherwise
excellent leaders ever sought to challenge Cultural Marxism in the citadels
of media, academia and entertainment).

The first area, however, that Cultural Marxists, like other totalitarians,
always seek to control is that of history. This is a lesson they have drawn

in particular from classical economic Marxism, which always makes one of its first priorities the revision of textbooks and educational materials to reflect Communist policy and ideology. The tendency within Communism to a 'Year Zero' mentality that erases all contradictory primary sources, physical evidence and conflicting interpretations of the past. as well as the evidence that supports these. reached perhaps its fullest expression under the regime of Pol Pot, but it is an instinct Cultural Marxists share. We have seen it manifested in demands for the renaming of buildings and streets that honour individuals Cultural Marxists wish to see erased from history, and in the desire to tear down statues that honour such individuals.

In the US, quite recently, various Civil War figures who fought for the South (including generals who actually supported the emancipation of slaves but resisted the North out of regional loyalty) have been attacked in this fashion, as well as traditional parades and celebrations such as Columbus Day. In Australia, a similar process has occurred, with Australia Day being targeted. In the UK, statues of Churchill or ones honouring Bomber Command in WWII have been defaced on multiple occasions, and even a restaurant that referenced Churchill in its decoration was targeted by militant activists. A mural at a British university including verses from Kipling has been destroyed, with none of the students involved facing any meaningful punishment for their vandalism.

This is all in accordance with an approach to history shared by Islamists who, just like Cultural Marxists, do wish to control history itself and every cultural expression of it. The Taliban blowing up gigantic Buddhist statues or the Islamic State's destruction of ancient Roman heritage sites is not qualitatively distinct from the Cultural Marxist's attitude to history. It differs only, thus far, in degree. The same barbarian philosophy of erasure, hatred and control motivates the self-righteous Western student activist and the black-clad Taliban savage. Indeed, it is part of the reason why they have so thoroughly aligned their interests and now work together in undermining the West.

Orwell, again, was one of the most prescient commentators on this aspect of Cultural Marxism before the term even existed. He stated: "The most effective way to destroy people is to deny and obliterate their own understanding of their history." This is the thread that unites all Cultural Marxist interactions with the history of Western civilisation. Seemingly diverse policies and actions like the growth of study areas devoted purely to non-Western writers and thinkers, the tendency of film makers to prioritise anti-Western or non-Western narratives, the decline of the study of Classics and classical history, the removal of Latin and Greek as signifiers of cultured attainment or serious scholarship, the protests towards and defacement or destruction of statues and busts deemed offensive, the pre-eminence of a Marxist reading of history, the concentration on Western sins and errors in school texts and syllabi, the removal of specifically nationalist, patriotic or Christian elements in teaching, the constant cudgel of 'diversity' in the judgement of quality of teaching by official bodies such as Ofsted in the UK (who have criticised certain schools for being 'too white'), are all part of the same agenda.

They are all attempts to control history and thereby control the future of the society in question. Those who write the past dominate the future. Cultural Marxists have understood this far better than their traditionalist opponents, who have often offered very little resistance, perhaps in the mistaken belief that the obvious advantages of Western civilisation are intel-lectually unassailable by more primitive forces, or through some vague hope that market forces will redress the balance and illustrate the absurdity of many Cultural Marxist positions.

25

CASE STUDY:
IMPERIAL SHADOWS, CULTURAL
MARXISM AND THE BRITISH EMPIRE

"When I was a girl, the idea that the British Empire
could ever end was absolutely inconceivable. And it
just disappeared, like all the other empires. You know,
when people talk about the British Empire, they always
forget that all the European countries had empires."

—Doris Lessing

THE BRITISH EMPIRE IS LONG SINCE DEAD, BUT
the habit of stamping on its grave still continues. South African stand up
comic Trevor Noah achieved greater notoriety and furthered his career
by incorporating a long skit on the Empire into his act and delivering it
to British audiences whilst on tour. The audience, composed primarily of
educated white professionals, dutifully laughed and applauded as a significant proportion of their national heritage was roundly mocked. Noah's take
was gentler than some others'. It was a sort of wistful mockery, the kind we
reserve for elderly relatives we don't respect. The gist of the argument was
'of course the Empire was an absurdity'. It was patently self-evident that the
architects of the Empire were pompous buffoons, motivated by an entirely

unjustified sense of racial superiority and happily exploiting large portions of the globe for no good reason whatsoever. The Empire wasn't so much evil, as it was ridiculous, and both audience and performer were united in the assumption that the British 'stole other people's land' and that the proper and fitting response to that was several generations of ridicule.

Noah's attitude, and that of his audience, did not emerge from a vacuum, but instead represents one of the gentler end points of a continuum of contempt for British history. Its origins begin before the Empire itself died, and what is now a sea of historical ignorance can be traced backwards to a few originating streams of socialist and anarchist critiques of imperialism. Comic self-mockery, always a strong trait of the English identity, plays its part too, evident in such diverse and otherwise dissimilar works as Lytton Strachey's *Eminent Victorians* and the Grossmith brothers' *The Diary of a Nobody*. Noah and his audience could be blissfully ignorant of details that contradict their understanding of the British imperial role in Africa, such as the work of colonial administrators and soldiers in ending the slave trade in Sudan or, in the case of Noah's South Africa, the far better native relations maintained by the British when compared with the attitudes and practices common to the Afrikaner settlers when dealing with Africans.

Anything which shows the Empire in a positive light has long since been suppressed. It was being suppressed even whilst the Empire was in its twilight years, and such knowledge is now cast in a perpetual darkness. Far from the Empire overshadowing post-colonial relations both within and between nations, it is truer to say that contemporary attitudes cast their shadow over the past, blotting out every imperial achievement and reducing some of the greatest figures of British history to the role of semi-comic villain.

The accepted status of the British imperial past as a shameful example of racist thinking combined with the exploitative nature of Western capitalist societies is a popular mainstay of much contemporary culture. Victim narratives from post-colonial sources are and have long been extremely popular, feeding into an ongoing resentment on the part of generations never ruled by anything remotely approaching a colonial master. Much of post-colonial literature presents either fictionalised or semi-autobiographical accounts framed around the inherent assumption of the invidious and malign nature of British imperial rule.

Chinua Achebe's *Things Fall Apart*, first published in 1958 by Heinemann, became the benchmark of artistic quality by which other such works were judged. Telling the story of Okonkwo, a prominent wrestling champion of a pre-colonial tribal society of the 1890s, the novel recounts the tragic consequences of the impact of an emerging colonial presence on native power structures, ideas of governance and masculinity, and on individuals like Okonkwo, who are ultimately destroyed by the new ways of doing things. It has sold more than 8 million copies and is taught as a standard text in schools throughout Africa as well as in post-colonial literature courses in almost all Western universities (I myself read it as part of my undergraduate reading list). Achebe himself has received some criticism from later generations of anti-imperialists for writing the novel in English and for adopting many of the literary conventions of the Western tradition, but the following assessment from Ernest N. Emenyonu represents the standard critical response:

"*Things Fall Apart* is indeed a classic study of cross-cultural misunderstanding and the consequences to the rest of humanity, when a belligerent culture or civilisation, out of sheer arrogance and ethnocentrism, takes it upon itself to invade another culture, another civilisation."

Here we see the assumptions of contemporary mainstream liberal attitudes underpinning each other, as both the 'ethnocentrism' and the 'arrogance' of British activities in Africa in the colonial period are assumed to be self-evident. Ethnocentrism as insult is itself a curious concept, in that it supposes that there is something fundamentally wrong in possessing a natural proclivity towards the culture within which one's own views have been formed, and selectively applies this natural feeling (common to all ethnic groups) as a negative trait somehow uniquely possessed by white Europeans. One might say in response that the comment mentions only a 'culture or civilisation', suggesting a universal condemnation of such attitudes, but when the only imperial projects ever discussed in this pejorative fashion are those of white Europeans, the bias becomes a little more evident.

When someone studies a post-colonial course in Western nations, they are not taught about other imperial projects and their consequences, such as the Japanese attempt to create an overseas empire in neighbouring oriental nations, or the imperial expansion of Ottoman power into Europe. Such wider contextualising of imperial ambitions might bring the awareness that all ethnic groups have engaged in such activity at one time or another, with greater and lesser degrees of nobility and barbarism in their motives and actions. Rather than this more nuanced understanding, students on such courses hear only about European, and primarily British, imperial excesses, from voices already convinced that the British Empire was an engine of oppression running on the fuel of prejudice.

White voices from within the critically acclaimed Western canon confirm exactly the same attitudes as black or brown voices do towards the cross-cultural interaction of Britain and the remainder of the world, with works like E.M. Forster's *A Passage to India* emphasising the callous stupidity of the imperial system which supposedly divided people on racial grounds. The fate of Dr Aziz, falsely accused of rape by hysterical white imperialists, is an interesting counterpoint to the story of Okonkwo. In both cases, a native society is shown to have been far more complex and precious than it was acknowledged to be, and a representative figure of that culture is unjustly destroyed by the ignorance and superstitions of the invading colonial masters.

Popular culture has not lagged behind highbrow literature in perpetuating these reductive stereotypes, although interestingly it is more commonly the case that popular manifestations of an anti-imperial historic grudge more often include the disaffected voices of white anti-imperialists and traditional alleged victims of English innate cruelty, such as the Irish or the Scots. The nationalist Irish myth of 700 years of continuous oppression from wicked England has in more recent years been critiqued by sophisticated historians like R.F. Foster (particularly in *The Irish Story: Telling Tales and Making it Up in Ireland*, a historical study so accurate it provoked the immediate contempt of Terry Eagleton in a Guardian review, always a sure sign of being right). Despite that, it has had enormous influence in popular culture and in Hollywood, where the instinctive belief in the evil of anything English ensures steady work as villains for British character actors, particularly those with a suitably old-fashioned plummy accent.

The grotesque abortion of history (and of narrative filmmaking) that was James Cameron's 1997 blockbuster, *Titanic*, is a typical example, depicting as it did a very easy, very distorted view of Anglo-Irish relations. The upstairs of the vessel is set aside for privileged boors and racist prudes, all possessed of titles and cut-glass Received Pronunciation English accents. The downstairs is where all the decent people can be found, all possessed of boundless *joi de vivre*, generosity of spirit, community feeling and compassionate empathy, hand in hand with foot stompingly vigorous dance moves. The Anglosphere upstairs is cold, cruel, artificial, greedy and ruthless. The Gaelosphere downstairs is warm, natural, generous and kind. Such crude propaganda, itself reflective of deeply racist anti-English and anti-British sentiments, purports to impose contemporary feel-good values on a significant maritime tragedy of the past. In doing so, it casually slandered many of the British crew who lost their lives trying to save others, even going so far as to depict one as a panicked gun-toting maniac, to the considerable distress of descendants and others aware of his actual self-sacrifice.

Impugning long dead servants of the Empire is an extremely effective short-cut to box office receipts, reflecting back at audiences the prejudices they have already been taught by Cultural Marxists in schools and universities. The beauty of the British Empire as bogeyman is that nobody remains who is likely to protest, since even the vast majority of right-wingers and traditionalists in the UK and elsewhere have a difficult time asserting any trenchant defence of imperialism. I'm not even attempting to do so myself, since my own view is coloured enough by contemporary attitudes to regard the Empire as essentially mistaken and all nations and peoples as possessing some right to self-determination. What I am noting, however, is the degree to which anti-imperialist narratives feed into the waters of ignorance, inundating more gullible minds with a soggy mess of second-rate ideas and unexamined prejudices.

Perhaps the most egregious example of the re-writing of history to conform to an anti-imperial, anti-British agenda came in Mel Gibson's millennial masterpiece of inaccuracy, *The Patriot*. Long before Gibson revealed his forthright racial thinking with drunken anti-Semitic outbursts, he had already displayed a consistent Antipodean chip on the shoulder with regard to the British. *The Patriot* forms a sort of cinematic trilogy of resentment with *Gallipoli* and *Braveheart* all confirming the ineradicable worthlessness of the British people in the eyes of the New-York-born Aussie action hero. In *The Patriot* we witness the full depravity of those vicious redcoats when innocent townsfolk are herded into a church and burned alive.

Of course, the trouble is that no such incident actually occurred in the American Revolutionary War. The incident seems to be a translocation of an SS atrocity in the French village of Ouradour-sur-Glane which actually occurred in 1944 during World War Two. A real Nazi atrocity is assigned to the British of the 1770s, whilst simultaneously whitewashing revolutionary figures of any controversial actions of their own. The British are so foul that even post-mortem desecration of their corpses by the protagonist is portrayed as a natural consequence of their oppressive rule. Again, this links in with US popular film attitudes to Nazis, with much the same trope featuring prominently in Quentin Tarantino's *Inglorious Bastards* (released 2009).

Some might say it is over-sensitive to object to such artistic licence with historical accuracy, since popular movies are intended to entertain rather than inform. The unfortunate truth, however, is that some of the highest-grossing movies of modern times show a consistent attitude towards the British which, if applied to almost any other nationality or ethnicity, would quickly be recognised as consistently racist negative stereotyping. Even the successes of the British in advancing and defending the freedom of others are subject to an appropriation which assigns them elsewhere, usually to fictional American heroes. The British capture of the Enigma device during WWII was transformed into an American success in *U571*, whilst *Saving Private Ryan* and *Band of Brothers* give the historically inaccurate impression that no British or Commonwealth troops took part in the D-Day landings.

We can therefore see a double-pronged assault on British history, with the evil being emphasised or inaccurately conflated with Nazism, whilst the good is ignored or assigned to become the achievements of others. Such depictions reach, collectively, a wider global audience than even the most successful critically acclaimed work of literature. For many who don't read for pleasure and don't study history in any true sense, the Hollywood caricatures may well form all they know of a significant period of British history. And the inaccuracy and distortion of these narratives is not even evident to many British observers, since they, too, have been raised, like post-colonial Americans or Irish or Nigerians or Indians, to see the height of British power as a period of unwavering oppression. Few Americans know that 100,000 of their countrymen were forced into exile at the end of the War of Independence, or that New York and many other places remained firmly Loyalist throughout the conflict. Few, if any, British people will have ever seen footage of Queen Victoria's Diamond Jubilee of 1897, or know that it was enthusiastically celebrated across the Empire, by many races and creeds, of whom the liberal contemporary assumption is that they were implacably opposed to British rule.

In the very same year that *The Patriot* reached a low point of cinematic anti-British racism, small 'c' conservative philosopher and critic Roger Scruton released *England, An Elegy*, one of the most moving personal accounts from the other side of the perspective. Scruton has long been a fierce and erudite champion of a more nuanced and reasoned approach to the legacy of Empire, and his own autobiographical account of growing up in a changing world is a melancholy but beautiful homage to much of our traditional landscape (both real and figurative) that has since been lost.

Scruton gives an account of the experience of one of his own schoolmasters who, like many others of the late nineteenth to early and mid-20th centuries, had served out a life of public service during the dying days of Britain's imperial presence. From personal experience, Scruton recounts the confusion and bewilderment of a generation prior to his own, who had been raised to still believe in the Empire and the good that it could achieve. Like the vast majority of colonial administrators and soldiers, we see a good man who strove to do his best in difficult circumstances, driven more by a sense of responsibility than by a desire to exploit others, and this is, although only one example, a far truer reflection of the nature of the imperial mission, as it was lived and enacted by the last generation to live through it, than the popular image of the cruel redcoat raping and enslaving defenceless victims. These were not men who were actively doing evil, but rather men who genuinely thought that they had been given a responsibility to bring peace, order, security, law, medicine, science, a beneficent religion and an improving commerce to all corners of the earth.

There is a level of ambition in that thinking which now appears to us as an engrained cultural and racial arrogance, but it was in many cases, and certainly by the late Empire, no more exclusive or supremacist than modern liberal assumptions, and in many cases far more humble and pragmatic. Intellectuals today rail about inequality, racism or white privilege from the comfortable sinecure of a university chair, whilst the missionaries of

Empire were travelling to the poorest regions of the globe and building roads, bridges, schools, wells and hospitals. It might be fair to ask which of those really does more good.

Misinformation regarding both the nature and the motivations of Britain's imperial past begins in our national curriculum, which at times seems more like a philosophy of self-loathing than an accurate summary of our history and of the cultural and artistic achievements of our ancestors. One of the richest historical heritages in the world is not even taught in a properly linear fashion. British children today are effectively robbed of their cultural inheritance, as the teaching syllabus jumps from the Romans in primary school to the Norman Conquest in Year Seven, at the start of secondary school. In one fell swoop, some six centuries of national history are swept aside, with no study of the Anglo-Saxons whatsoever. Crucially, the period which receives the least attention in the national curriculum framework for British schools is the very same period in which the identity and ethnicity of the English is forged. The political geography of our land, the counties we inhabit today, were determined in this period as Anglo Saxon kingdoms. Our law was codified by Alfred the Great, our survival as a people dependent on the efforts of Alfred and his descendants, and our church gradually developed and matured in the same six turbulent centuries.

English identity is inextricably linked to this period, and no true under-standing of our nation can be formed without a familiarity with its birth. Our national epic poem, *Beowulf*, is not automatically studied, and as both pupil and teacher I can never recall encountering it. The works of the Venerable Bede, or the accounts of *The Anglo Saxon Chronicle*, would with equivalent antiquity and importance in other cultures form a key part of the educational process, giving those who encountered them a firm sense of the rich heritage of their identity. In British schools, both students and the majority of the teachers are blissfully unaware of their existence. No doubt some could point to a national curriculum framework document citing the inclusion of such things. Few, however, could tell us of the lesson in which an encounter with the formative texts and artefacts of English identity ever occurred. Several other significant gaps break the narrative of the teaching of our history. Rather like presenting a novel from which key chapters have been ripped, students are left with a confused impression of random events devoid of cause and effect, events which have no natural connection with their own lives and the reality they inhabit.

For the British themselves, the psychological roots of the contemporary attitude of disdain towards the imperial past are rather obvious, whilst the reasoning of those from post-colonial nations is also easy to comprehend. Contemporary politicians and individuals, both at home and abroad, are excused from facing the difficult reality that their own poor choices since the death of Empire may have more to do with the inequalities and injustices present today than the actions of imperial administrators several generations ago. The record of many post-colonial nations in the management of their affairs after independence is not a proud one, although it is an oft-neglected fact that the departing British authorities did in many cases strive mightily to leave in place the institutions, freedoms and structures of governance that had cemented Britain's prior success.

The near-bankrupt Britain that retreated from imperial power in the mid-20th century was in fact deeply concerned with doing so in as responsible a manner as possible. A separation of church and state, a parliamentary multi-party system, a crowned figurehead acting as a static check on the ambitions of politicians and a symbol of unity regardless of caste or creed, a connection with a wide range of trading partners, a judicial system independent of government, all of these things were passed on as best as the dying Empire could manage. These, together with an infrastructure of government buildings, railways, roads, schools, hospitals, missions, ports and, in some cases, vastly expanded or newly created cities, were the true imperial legacy, more real, more concrete and more beneficial than any of the supposed psychic scars also left behind.

It is not the fault of the British that figures like Idi Amin, trained in the British Army, busily set about destroying the stabilising, peaceful social structures bequeathed to them and erecting barbaric dictatorships instead. Or if we look at Robert Mugabe and his ZANU party in Zimbabwe, we see that it is a post-colonial grievance policy of forced land redistribution, political corruption and ineffective management under effective dictatorship that has turned the former breadbasket of Africa into a basket case of economic and moral decline. Anti-colonialists, trained only in the assumptive rhetoric of blaming Britain for every disaster of their own making, often have little idea how to govern either effectively or fairly. As each new disaster confirms their own lack of genuine leadership qualities, the rhetoric of abuse aimed at the imperial past increases, like a petulant individual, long into adulthood, blaming their own criminality on a difficult relationship with a parent.

The British attitude to their imperial past also offers this comforting excuse, as contemporary liberals can vindicate their moral superiority by joining in post-colonial condemnations of their own heritage. Rather like white liberals spreading the racist mantra of white privilege, British leaders openly sympathise with the most inaccurate assessments of the imperial political legacy. The crisis of confidence in Western values and civilisation generally, provoked by the tremendous suffering and the obvious barbarities of the two world wars, feed into this *mea culpa* narrative. Tony Blair rarely encountered an ancient grievance which he wasn't prepared to publicly apologise for, having had as little to do with it as any other modern British person. Such revisionist moments of self-abasement as his public apology to Ghanaian President John Agyekum Kufuor shortly before the 200th anniversary of the abolition of slavery nurtured the impression that slavery — an institution practised by every race over thousands of years of human history — was a uniquely British invention of subjugation or that the British, one of the very first modern nations to outlaw the practice and one of the most vigorous international opponents of it thereafter, still had some ineradicable permanent racial guilt to bear for it today.

This attitude of quick and easy apologies for things for which he bore no responsibility always contrasted strongly with Blair's trenchant refusal to ever apologise for things for which he was personally responsible, like lying to Parliament and the public in order to pursue a war with their deceived support. The nominally Conservative PM David Cameron joined the ritual abasement brigade in February 2013, when he apologised for the 1919 Amritsar Massacre, describing it as a "deeply shameful event in British history". Perhaps that assessment is accurate, but staunch imperialists of the time, including Churchill, had condemned the event when it occurred. It therefore seems, to a rational observer, a bizarre incident to have a PM a century later have to go through the process of apologising again. Current Canadian PM Justin Trudeau has repeatedly apologised for things which no contemporary Canadian can be considered guilty of, and this process of apologising to people who have never been personally oppressed on behalf of people who are long dead is sadly commonplace in the West as a whole. The same logic would have us demanding an apology from the Danish ambassador for the terrible slaughter of monks at Lindisfarne in 793AD.

When one is actually aware of the nature of the British Empire, the reality of historical events often contradicts the now almost universally accepted tale of oppression, racism and self-interested greed. The best concise expression of the manner in which the Empire was acquired remains John Robert Seeley's famous quote from his 1883 defence of the imperial project, or rather lack of project, *The Expansion of England*, when he stated "we seem, as it were, to have conquered half the world in a fit of absence of mind". The piecemeal expansion of Empire, the pivotal role played by individual adventurers such as Cecil Rhodes, the essentially mercantile nature of colonialism spread by businesses such as the East India Company, all confirm the truth of an assertion now wilfully ignored by the apparent belief that the Empire was the result of an active and continuous racial malice over the course of three centuries. And this expansion by accident might also be justifiably applied to the history of those darker moments of imperial British history that now feature as the only aspects of it taught or remembered in both formal schooling and popular culture.

A modern liberal, for example, might know enough to glibly state that the British invented concentration camps, ignoring the deeper truth that the term as applied to the policies enacted during the Boer War had no relation to the term as it is used today. A misguided idea designed to reduce the ease with which British troops were being killed by Boer marksman able to hide within sympathetic Boer villages is equated with deliberate factories of death designed to eliminate entire populations, whilst tragic and shocking casualty figures caused entirely accidentally by overcrowding and unexpected disease are assumed to be morally parallel with planned genocide. Events like the Amritsar Massacre or, post-Empire but within a post-colonial context, a tragedy such as Bloody Sunday, are shocking precisely because the British do not engage in deliberate civilian slaughter, do follow civilised rules of conduct, and have never engaged in the kind of planned, widescale, engineered murder which distinguishes actual evil regimes (such as is seen far more often amongst anti-imperialist, communist or post-colonial nations than was witnessed from any British source at any point in history).

No figure like Gandhi, following a policy of purely peaceful protest, could have had the same impact against, say, Soviet Russia, Communist China, Tsarist Russia or Imperial Japan. It is perhaps most illustrative of the true nature of Britain's imperial past if we compare the Pax Britannica with the Rape of Nanking or the Nazi policy of *lebensraum* or Leopold II's administration of the Congo. No such descent into barbarity can be assigned to British rule. Imperfect, misguided, full of noble intent and unintended consequence, acquired by accident and lost by design, the British Empire was a quixotic reflection of the British character itself in its most confident phase. Without it, the British would never have had sufficient strength and resources to be able to defeat genuine tyrannical evils, from Napoleon to Kaiser Wilhelm to Hitler and Stalin. The legacy of Empire is one which has shaped a world more free than that which would have existed without it.

How then do these issues raised above, the difference between the reality of a generally benevolent imperial legacy contrasted with the widespread belief in the evil nature of British history, relate to our central theme of Cultural Marxism? They do so, of course, by justifying the subordination of British interests to Cultural Marxist agendas in our own society today, and by supporting a one-sided grievance rhetoric that both demonises and excludes modern British citizens. Whether it is a call for reparations for slavery from African or Jamaican politicians, or a ludicrous campaign of vandalism directed at a statue of Rhodes, or Indian or Pakistani demands for the repatriation of part of the Crown Jewels, a British citizen is only ever told that his nation owes something to others, and that he is at some sort of undying moral deficit with an equivalent person in any other nation.

And all of this burden of racial guilt has a contemporary purpose. By putting British people who have never been part of imperialism in the role of inherited imperial scapegoat, the political exclusion of native British people, both at home and on the world stage, becomes that much easier. Not only are they deprived of their history, and presented with a sort of ugly changeling version of it, they must also concede more and more today on the basis of assumed crimes committed many years ago. And this has an effect in almost every political sphere we can mention.

One might think that reactions to climate change, for example, would be based on scientific evidence followed by shared international responses. Instead, we see rapidly industrialising nations asserting that they have some sort of right to pollute the planet today because Britain industrialised first, when nobody had any scientific understanding of the consequences of carbon dioxide emissions. We see Indian politicians and scientists describing British calls for greater ecological responsibility as a form of imperialism, and demanding payments from the British to act in a way conducive to the wellbeing of the entire planet. The Paris Agreement, which President Trump was roundly condemned for rejecting, actually embodied this post-colonial guilt, as Western nations were expected to pay for past pollution whilst developing nations are allowed to expand pollution. Britain, of course, joined the condemnation of Trump's decision, with little thought to the possibility that it might have some rational basis. This is, after all, how Britain has been taught to think by Cultural Marxists. The West must pay, today, for its history, while the rest of the world can enact, today, various forms of selfishness with complete impunity.

26

Cultural Marxism in Action: The War Against Brexit

2016 PRESENTED THE WORLD WITH TWO ENTIRELY
unexpected political results: the election of Trump and the British vote to withdraw from the European Union. In both cases, the mainstream consensus, guided by a Cultural Marxist reading of history and that sense of inevitable progressive triumph contemporary liberals share with other essentially religiously minded fanatics, had considered these results impossible. On the eve of the UK referendum in 2016, professional pollsters confidently asserted that Remain had an unassailable ten-point lead. US readers will be familiar with similar inaccurate polling prior to Trump's election, as well as the constant scorn and derision poured upon anyone independent-minded enough to predict otherwise (Anne Coulter, for example).

In Britain, the horror of the political Establishment at the result of the referendum was evident even in the process of declaring the result. The BBC was typical of mainstream news channels in entering into an immediate sombre mood of non- reflection, in which astonishment that their own prejudices were not held by others was far more important to report than anything else. It was like an Islington dinner party at which a guest had arrived with a supermarket-brand bottle of wine. Gasps of horror were the order of the day. Those watching were treated to three days of 'my god, how awful', little realising that this would segue effortlessly into three years of the same. It is sad to report that I know this to be the case from being foolish enough to watch the coverage. Guest after guest, commentator after commentator, was presented to describe the shock, hurt, anger and loss of having a democratic vote go against their wishes. Interviews became tearful, as if after some natural catastrophe — the explosion of a volcano, perhaps, which nobody had known existed in the middle of England. The terrifying roar of a tsunami, with each scratch of a pen on a ballot paper being another little wave in the towering wall of water washing away the structures of European rule from the shores of the British isles.

We should have known, of course. We, the majority who voted to leave and always understood what it meant, should have known what was actually coming. People who find your freedom horrific never release your chains, not unless you point a gun at them and demand it. Because those who despised Brexit and the kind of people who voted for it with every fibre of their beings were never going to just let it happen. They were never going to respect the result. They were never going to allow normal democratic practice to stand in their way. These, the Remain side, were the rich and the powerful. Brexit was such a horrific shock to them precisely because they had got their way, despite a supposed democracy consisting of more people like us than like them, for 70 years. These are the people who had constructed the post-war consensus, who ruled both main parties, who controlled every media organisation and every cultural and social institution of note in the country. Most importantly, as developments much later would show, they already owned the Speaker of the House of Commons and at least 70% of the Parliament in Westminster.

The initial stirrings of their resistance to this unwelcome intrusion of direct democracy on political decision-making in the UK manifested themselves in the media choice to concentrate solely on the reactions of the losing side of the debate. The reality that millions of people were joyously delighted with the result could not be shared, for that would legitimise the result itself and show Brexit from the beginning in a positive light. It's a moot point to question how conscious this decision was. The media class were in shock, and it may have merely been the kind of thing that happens when people start urgently discussing amongst themselves an event which for them was entirely unhappy. Of course, this discussion dominated the airwaves and the TV studios, seizing hold of every radio commentary and every news item, simply because the radio, TV and newspaper professionals were almost all on the side of Remain.

But it cannot have been long before this media concentration on one side of things, one way of viewing Brexit, moved from confirmation bias to deliberate conspiracy. The enormous disparity on air in the number of responses between the Leave and Remain sides testifies to conscious deception rather than anything else. Even a subconscious bias could not so totally remove Leave voices from the debate, for in the past three years the only sources of consistent Leave opinion have been coming from the non-mainstream office of Spiked and the no doubt plusher but rather old-fashioned offices of The Telegraph. It is worth noting that even key media outlets with a long history of Euroscepticism, that is places where a celebration of Brexit might be expected and some rational discourse on the positive democratic and economic features of it discussed, have in the course of the last three years been seized by fanatical adherents of Remain. First, the disgraced ex-Chancellor George Osborne, on the back of some minor journalistic experience thirty years previously, was parachuted in to take command of The Evening Standard. Then, long-standing Eurosceptic Daily Mail editor Paul Dacre was conveniently retired, and the helm of the Mail handed to a rabidly pro-European replacement.

Despite the repeated Cultural Marxist claim that the British media is fanatically right-wing (this has always ignored the news and entertainment market share of the BBC on radio and television, far broader in audience than the 'Murdoch press'), these seizures of just two newspaper editorships ensured an almost clean sweep of pro-Remain news coverage in the UK. Since Murdoch's own withdrawal from the British political scene following the bruising after effects of an entirely different controversy (the hacking scandal that ended the News of the World), what remained of British right-wing media content began the saga of Brexit from a position of meek caution. Once powerful engines of public opinion like The Sun and The Mail have either joined the other side or been too ineffectual to land any blows during the battle. The kind of populist Eurosceptic sentiment that is felt by most of the working class has had no vocal media champions save for Spiked (arguing from the almost vanished phenomenon of an articulate, rational and patriotic Left) and The Express (taking up the mantle of champion of patriotic blue-collar man abandoned by The Sun).

TV media, which is now far more influential than the archaic medium of print, has been wholly Remain, arguing consistently, stridently and quite often hysterically from a Remain perspective. The BBC, ITV, C4, etc. have been careful to maintain some thin semblance of balance by every now and then letting a Leave representative talk. But look at how they all do this. In each case, any Leave speaker will be surrounded by a panel of Remain opponents, always outnumbered if seldom intellectually outgunned. The relentless Project Fear campaign first initiated by the Remain efforts of the Cameron government has of course never relented and has been given almost every moment of available airtime. We have become used to the words 'may', 'could' and 'might' being used as if they meant 'will', 'shall' and 'already have' in presentations of doom-laden scenarios that are always purely speculative, evidence-free suggestions of just how bad a real Brexit might be. Predicted economic doom from Remain Treasury forecasts (already halved in catastrophe level, which of course nobody has commented on as potentially invalidating them entirely) have taken the role of religious oracle, and the British TV media have been wildly evangelical in their desire to spread these unsubstantiated claims.

Cultural Marxists, of course, have no respect for the traditional values or objective standards of reporting that would give pause to this scandalously one-sided coverage of Brexit. Truth is always their first victim, slain alongside Reason and Balance, Logic and Objectivity. Reporters steeped in Cultural Marxist attitudes have not sifted positive and negative implications of Brexit in order to ascertain a rational, balanced view to present to the public. Rather, they have proselytised doom, selectively ignored all positive arguments, and obsessively dissected and disseminated any and all negative comment they can find. This has led to some extraordinary examples of biased focus. Obscure warnings from the sandwich-making industry about a possible dearth of lettuce have been pondered with grim intent as potential signs of the impending Brexit apocalypse, whereas the rather more serious warning from a former head of the Armed Forces and a former head of MI6 regarding the security implications of Theresa May's Withdrawal Agreement passed with almost no comment on TV, radio or in most newspapers. Despite boasting of their love for expert informed analysis, and despite their assumption that all the experts on geopolitics are on their side, most Remain advocates would still rather listen to Gary Lineker telling us how wonderful the EU is than take a former head of MI6 at his word regarding the security implications of being ruled from abroad. Expertise, it seems, is only expert insofar as it is Remain.

The absurdity and hysteria of Remain thinking leaves one constantly wondering how much of it can be classed as malign dishonesty and how much should be thought of instead as unfortunate psychosis. It is difficult, for example, to communicate in any rational way with people who worry more about the availability of Swiss cheese than they do about the continuation of democratic structures of government. What do you say to persuade a person who is intensely terrified of the prospect of standing in a different queue when they go on holiday, or who seriously believes that air travel between the UK and Europe is in danger of ceasing unless we accept continued EU regulation of our trade? How do you talk to a person, even an expert in the field, who seriously thinks that the EU would be insane enough to hold up vital cancer medicines in unnecessary border delays, but at the same time argues that we should keep being ruled by these Cancer-Loving bureaucrats? Despite all the intransigence and malice of the EU I still have difficulty picturing them deliberately stopping cancer treatments, and yet some of their strongest supporters do not. Nor do they see what such a view says about the EU, or about them.

Only one thing is more astonishing than the absurdity of the fears which Remain panders to, and that is the degree to which these fears have controlled the narrative of Brexit. The story of Brexit has been the tale of how a rational, positive move towards greater enfranchisement and liberty has been turned into an irrational chorus of fear, and the fear has triumphed. It has not triumphed in the hearts of the stubbornly rational and pragmatic Leave voter, of course, for these people being mainly working class deal with real life in a more visceral sense than their often privileged opponents. They are not so easily swayed by fainting spells and operatic shrieks, and still tend to view such things with a dash of manly disdain. It has persuaded those who were already looking to be persuaded, the defeated Remain voters and the defeated British political Establishment. But these people are the ones in positions of power already.

In recent years, one of the most successful and long-running British TV shows was a paranormal investigation programme called Most Haunted. It ran for hundreds of episodes and gained excellent viewing figures on a range of different channels. Every episode followed exactly the same format. A team of investigators would descend upon a supposedly haunted location, accompanied by an alleged medium. The team would wander around the abandoned property in the dark, bumping into things, whispering into the camera, and telling us about sudden fluctuations in temperature we had no way of verifying ourselves. Various bumps and creaks would be explained as the actions of ghosts or spirits trying to communicate with the team, and they would either encourage one another to start screaming or give the medium an opportunity to consult some fictional spirit guide or even contact the unproven entities said to be swirling around at that moment. Having whipped each other up into frenzies of fear or strange little mono-logues about imaginary troubles, the team would conclude that definitive proof of the supernatural had been obtained. After all, we would not just scream at nothing, would we?

Mainstream commentary on Brexit has followed exactly the same format as an episode of Most Haunted. Brave teams of Remain politicians, jour-nalists and commentators have investigated the horrific scene of their own democratic defeat, Britain, and thoroughly examined it for supernatural explanations of that defeat. They have conjured spirits and consulted ghosts, huddled around ouija boards. "Are EU there still? Will EU come back to us? Why did they kill EU?". They have projected their fears onto the political scene, let them run loose in the haunted House of Commons, and declared that the hellish visions thus displayed will surely consume us all unless we reverse Brexit. Brexit, you see, was the sinful enquiry, the guilty act that is often found at the beginning of horror stories. But it can be dispelled. We don't have to face the horrors. We can have a second referendum, or revoke Article 50, or remain in a customs union. We, assert our fearful politicians, would not scream at nothing, would we?

Just think of how irrational this war on Brexit has been, how ludicrous the fears it represents, and the Most Haunted analogy becomes ever more convincing. Key Remain arguments are both religious and supernatural. They are displays of magical thinking. They believe in mind-reading powers. 'You didn't know what you were voting for' they say. How could they know that for 17.4 million people who quite obviously think differently from them? They can tell us what we were thinking in 2016, our emotional and psychological state in the privacy of the voting booth. They know, purely by mind-reading powers, that many of us are racists. They believe in prophecy. Of course they call it economics, but it is still prophecy.

'Brexit will destroy our future prosperity' they scream, as if there would not be after Brexit the same responsibility to shape a future rather than just passively suffer it. They carefully model economic scenarios in which future governments take no mitigating actions whatsoever, sign no new trade deals having obtained the ability to do so, find not one positive economic boon from fully controlling our own economic choices. And they present these mystical speculations as evidence, as fact, as documents from a future seen only in their visions. They crash into walls in the darkness, scream, and insist that these are supernatural blows. They run into those walls in a blind panic, and then blame the resulting bruises on that malevolent spirit, Brexit.

Perhaps this seems like mere hyperbole or rhetoric. It is not. There has been a genuinely disturbed reaction to Brexit, a psychologically damaged reaction from the side claiming to be rational, authoritative, expert and sensible. Just like Trump Derangement Syndrome, the distorting effect of a Cultural Marxist media campaign of fear has been to render a significant proportion of the populace clinically insane on an important political topic that should be dealt with in a far calmer manner. Nobody who has heard Remain supporters screaming in the background of TV reports, weeping hysterically or painting themselves blue can consider all aspects of Remain thinking rational or measured. Evan Davies on BBC Radio Four even recently did a segment describing the 'devastating' psychological impact of Brexit. That is, people claiming to have experienced extreme stress and mental anguish on the basis that other people voted differently to them.

The things to which this hysterical reaction is applied measure the growth of the Remain fight-back against a democratic result. Their fear and their confidence, oddly, go hand in hand. The more they are confident of being able to reassert control and ditch democracy, the more fearful the visions they paint of not doing so. The more hysterical their beliefs regarding the nature of Brexit, the more firmly they seize control over the political institutions and processes charged by the public with delivering it. A madman will seize control of the steering wheel from the backseat if the driver goes in a direction that they do not like.

A referendum, of course, switches seats in an orderly fashion. The driver becomes the public, rather than the political class claiming to represent the public. This is precisely why referendums are normally disliked and opposed by mainstream politicians in the first place. Now the 'professional' is seizing the wheel again. We were steering towards national sovereignty and individual liberty. This has not been the direction of travel of the last 50 years, not the direction of travel familiar to those used to guiding our nation, and not a direction that anyone raised in a Cultural Marxist attitude of total hatred of the nation state can tolerate.

We should perhaps remind ourselves of what it is that Cultural Marxists, the EU, and the middle class supporters of Remain all fear. They fear the nation state, of course, and prefer globalist bureaucratic alternatives. They fear losing control and power, perks and privilege. The EU declares in a prominent plaque that nation states are the source of all the evils that have bedevilled mankind. Macron and Merkel both denounce nationalism. But this is, ultimately, still a code. They do not fear nation states that are compliant, or national institutions that accept international direction. They do not fear the professional political and media class in any given nation state, because they are assured that these share their aims and prejudices. Ultimately what they fear is you. The great unwashed. The revolting masses. The working class. The British and European public, or at least, all those parts of the public not already bribed or bullied into abject subservience. They fear you, and they hate you, and we see this quite clearly in the kinds of slogans painted on the placards of Remain campaigners or expressed in the logic of key Remain arguments.

We can also contrast all this with the actuality, with genuine objective facts regarding what Brexit is and how it would look. The former Australian PM Tony Abbott succinctly and accurately described what a Brexit Britain would actually look like. Politically and economically, it would look like a Canada, or an Australia, or a New Zealand. It would, like Australia, trade with the EU under WTO terms. That is the great fear, the great post-apocalyptic horror we have seen described as 'plunging into the abyss' or 'crashing out' or 'going over a cliff edge'. Trading under internationally agreed guidelines designed to facilitate free trade. Acquiring the power to remove burdensome tariffs on non-EU goods, obtaining cheaper food, clothing and basic materials currently subject to those punitive, protectionist EU measures. Shifting our focus to the global markets where 90% of all future growth, it has been predicted, will occur. And at what cost? At the cost of tariffs on some EU goods, to be sure. But ones limited by WTO guidelines and by the obvious fact that we would be the EU's largest external market. How many sellers ultimately decide to punish their customers? And what happens to them when they do?

The great glaring actuality is that most nations on Earth are independent, sovereign nation states. Tiny Singapore is such, and somehow manages to thrive. But the utterly irrational Remain position, the starting assumption, is that Britain, uniquely, cannot reclaim this independence. The 5th largest economy in the world, the financial capital of the world, the second-greatest service provider in the world, the second-greatest soft power exponents in the world and still one of the great military powers in the world, cannot rule itself without economic catastrophe. That is the argument, that is the fear, that is the assumption underpinning every other Remain point. It is the lifeblood of every doom forecast, and it is pure, unadulterated horseshit contradicted by the living experience of a thousand years of our own history and the current status of nearly every other non-EU nation on Earth.

For this lie, this absurd fear, you are asked to sacrifice your freedom, your very democracy. You are asked to exchange the right to have your vote honoured and the right to national self-determination, both things for which previous generations have been prepared to die, because some businesses trading with the EU do not want to fill in a customs form or see a 2 or 3% increase in the price of a component they source from the EU. Some students don't want to fill in a ten-minute visa application form to spend six months in Europe. Some middle-class families are worried that they would have difficulty obtaining foreign nannies. One Remain placard, representative of all this nonsense, whined that Gucci would become more expensive. And these are the reasons for which you should accept foreign rule without representation, apparently.

So the war against Brexit begins from an enormous lie, and proceeds via a series of absurdities. But for all the obvious idiocy of the fears on which it is based, the methods by which these fear-crazed fanatics have assumed control of the Brexit process are anything but cowardly. There is a curious juxtaposition here. Remainers have been terrified sheep in their ideas regarding Britain's natural position in the world, but ravenous lions in their attempts to seize Britain by the scruff of the neck and direct its policy. Brexiteers, by contrast, have a bold and confident vision of Britain's future. Politics is often dominated by the weak because cowards are more ruthless than heroes.

Look at the direction of travel. In the immediate aftermath of the 2016 vote, Leave was buoyant and Remain deflated. Both main parties declared that they would honour the result. MPs voted by an overwhelming majority to do so. When May decided to call a snap election, both main parties declared that they would enact Brexit. Every single MP in those parties, including the most zealous Remain partisans like Anna Soubry, Dominic Grieve, Hilary Benn, Ken Clarke, Keir Starmer, all stood on manifestos pledging to honour the result. May gave speeches indicating a total commitment to delivering the result. In the referendum itself, David Cameron declared in a televised national address exactly what the referendum was voting on. He said that it meant leaving the Single Market, leaving the Customs Union and leaving all EU authority over our law and trade. He said it was a decision for the people that would be honoured, and that it was our choice, not the choice of Parliament. All MPs in all parties were aware of that. All members of the public voting were or should have been aware of that.

Thus, when Cameron suddenly resigned, the Leave voting public might have expected to see a prominent Leave figure assume office. Instead, they saw a Remain PM and a Remain Chancellor. They saw an illusion of pursuing Brexit, followed by a Civil Service coup delivering a Remain deal. And today we are seeing all forms of real Brexit honouring the 2016 referendum excluded by the Parliament that was supposed to have given the decision to us. Today we see a full Customs Union looking like the most likely outcome. The Cultural Marxist narrative of fear and the typical Cultural Marxist seizure of the levers of power, has destroyed any real prospect of Brexit being delivered, unless by some slim possibility the EU itself ends up forcing a 'no deal' out of sheer petulance.

The war against Brexit was, and is, a war against accountable democracy. For if one vote, the largest vote in our history, can simply be set aside by a middle class that does not wish to see it happen and a ruling class that controls the institutions tasked with delivering it, than any vote can be set aside. Votes become conditional not on who wins that vote but on the relative power of the winning and losing sides. As Charles II warned when Parliament seized power from the Crown, it simply becomes a matter of who is the greater brigand. The same applies when Parliament seizes power from the people, or forgets that the sovereignty of Parliament exists only by the consent of the people and only for the essential purpose of preserving the orderly management of a sovereign state. Ultimately, it is a war against you, the voter, waged by your elected and unelected rulers.

It is also illustrative of our central theme of Cultural Marxism. Only a nation in which Cultural Marxism has already taught the majority of the ruling class to hate their own history, their own people, their own nation, could the sophistries and absurdities of Remain reasoning be widely accepted. Only Cultural Marxists could declare they are being patriotic by forcing their fellow citizens to remain under foreign rule. Only those schooled in the moral relativism of Cultural Marxism could accept disenfranchising 17.4 million of their fellow citizens with the brazen declaration that doing so represents 'more' democracy. Only in a nation in which the Cultural Marxist long march through the institutions has already established a firm control over the media, the State broadcaster, the Parliament, the Speakership, the Cabinet, the Civil Service and the main political parties could a vote like the 2016 referendum be effectively reversed, using the very institutions supposed to defend the nation as the means of the nation's suppression.

27

Cultural Marxism in Action: The War Against Trump

DONALD TRUMP WAS NOT ALWAYS A MONSTER. He was a hugely successful businessman. He was an embodiment of the American Dream. He was a television personality, wholesome enough to make cameo appearances in films like Home Alone and popular enough to headline the US version of The Apprentice. He was the descendant of immigrants, and a champion of black rights. He was recognised with an award for this at an event attended by, amongst others, Mohammed Ali. He was photographed smiling with the daughter of Martin Luther King, with Jesse Jackson, with the Clintons. Hilary declared that America needed more men like Donald Trump involved in politics. Oprah pressed him to make a Presidential run, opining in as many words that he had all the qualities required of a President. Trump modestly, and somewhat uncharacteristically, demurred. Despite a colourful personal life involving several marriages, he had never been accused of misogyny, of contempt for women, or of sexual abuse, and was not surrounded, unlike other prominent Democrats, by lifelong rumours of such.

Nor was Donald Trump a warmonger, or someone likely to create World War Three. He had opposed several US foreign policy blunders. He had argued against the Second Iraq War and the interventions in Afghanistan, and consistently favoured a non interventionist strategy more likely to be popular with the Left rather than the Right of US politics. He had been interviewed several times on these topics, and always held to a consistent and rational distaste for military adventures with no sign of direct benefit to the US people, and every sign of encouraging negative global responses to US power. He had argued that the US military existed to protect US interests rather than spread US ideology, to be reactive rather than proactive, to contain and eliminate genuine threats rather than to by excessive belligerence create new ones.

Donald Trump became a monster the moment that he stopped being a member of the Democratic Party. He became a monster not because his nature or his views changed or because his personality and mannerisms were suddenly revealed, but because he defied the power of the Democratic Party and, even worse, started to defy the assumptions on which that power rests. If there is one thing that those who love and those who hate Trump can surely agree on it is that he makes no effort to disguise his nature. He is not a smooth political operator. He does not say one thing in public and the opposite in private. He does not promise to do that which he has no intention of doing. If he did, he would have given up on most of his policy platform a long time ago. He speaks to a journalist or an interviewer or a rally the same way he always speaks, disguising nothing. In this sense, despite repeatedly being called a liar, he is the most honest person to enter US politics since George Washington, a boast equal to Trump's bombastic self assessments but one that happens to be true. If he is a monster now, he was always a monster, and all those Democrats who praised him must have known it, too. A man like Trump does not hide what he is.

This is not to say that Trump is not a flawed human being, as fallible as the rest of us, sometimes moreso, and sometimes less so. Nobody who voted for Trump, or intends to do so again, is unaware of his flaws. The war against Trump consists of repeating things both his supporters and detractors already know. We know that his hair looks strange. He knows it too. Everyone knows it. For some reason many of us have decided that hairstyle is not the basis on which to select the leader of the free world. We know that he has small hands, and likewise cannot fathom why that should matter, despite its huge significance to liberal sketchwriters. More importantly, we know that he can be crude, and rude, and aggressive, that he mocks people he doesn't like, that he holds burning grudges, that he is extraordinarily thin skinned at times, that he has an enormous ego and constantly boasts about his own achievements. We know that he eats fast food, tweets constantly, can be physically awkward or verbally clumsy. We know that his speech patterns are easy to ridicule.

Those who hate him seem to think that those who don't are unaware of these traits and personality flaws. The idea that we could be aware of them, and still prefer his crude honesty to smooth deceptions, seems beyond the ability of liberals to fathom. The idea that we should examine his actions and policies, and note that they have not contained any of the horrors ascribed to him and are in fact consistent with traditional, classical liberal values does not occur to the hysterical liberal reaction to him. Confronted with our inability to share their hysteria, the tactic of the anti Trump fanatic has simply been to scream louder, weep harder, and threaten us with violence. These acts, supposedly, are designed to convince us that Trump is a threat to our sanity and safety, rather than the person screaming in our faces.

Perhaps the most idiotic charge to level against Trump is that he is a vainglorious narcissist, that he has a boundless ego. These are hardly character traits unlikely to develop in a billionaire or a TV star or a business magnate. For the individual that is all three, they are probably unavoidable requirements of getting to that position. The same applies to every single significant political candidate, especially those that aspire to the Presidency. Wasn't it a monstrous act of ego for an obscure community organiser who had barely held any significant post to aspire to the presidency? Or for him to accept a Nobel Prize before actually doing anything? Or for him to claim to embody abstract concepts like 'hope' and 'change' and 'the will to dream'? Does anyone seriously suppose that Obama's ego is any less expansive than that of Donald Trump?

Similarly, when Al Gore decided that he could, in a single video, single handedly persuade the globe to adopt greener policies, was that not just a little bit egotistical? When Hollywood celebrities lecture us on how we should think, who we should hate, and why we should oppose Trump they do so with far less mandate, less political experience and less appeal to real Americans than Trump himself possesses. But are these not attempts to impose their ego on the political destiny of their nation? More recently, does that darling of the American Left, Ocasio-Cortez, display a certainty of ego far beyond her years or actual accomplishments? When she along with other newly elected overly hyped leftist females posed for a succession of photo shoots were they not revelling in the attention and power like giddy princesses drunk on political fame?

In Britain after the Brexit referendum an event took on symbolic import as it became loaded with all the meanings associated with a clear, visible rejection of the Cultural Marxist agenda. In the US a person became a symbol, as had frequently been the case in a culture that from its outset has seemed to function via a Carlyle inspired belief in the absolute reality of heroes. From Washington to Hamilton to Lincoln to JFK, Americans have always been very ready to invest key figures with a symbolic meaning far beyond their status as powerful individuals. It is no accident that it was Americans who invented the superhero and the supervillain, and there is a strong element of the comic book in both positive and negative reactions to Trump. It's curious that a nation that began by rejecting the traditional symbol of kingship should confer a kind of monarchy on others, on the role of POTUS, on great leaders, on musicians like Elvis or sportsmen like Babe Ruth, inventing modern celebrity in the process. Resolutely unimpressed by a King, but always ready to unofficially crown a King of Rock n' Roll, a King of Pop or a 'Leader of the Free World' (without asking the rest of us first).

If Americans were culturally conditioned to invest individuals with symbolic meaning, Trump was constitutionally fitted to the role. Both his flaws and his strengths are characteristically American ones. The reason he is beloved by many is because of how much he does indeed represent them, not just the politics they wish to see enacted, but the way in which that politics is delivered. And he is hated for the same reasons, for how perfectly he summarises in one person the divisions, the contradictions, the beauty and the ugliness of America itself. Whilst his foreign policy instincts may be surprisingly far less bellicose than those of his liberal haters, his manner of forthrightly declaring some nations to be shitholes resonates with both admirers and opponents more than the policies themselves. Lovers know the statement to be true, and admire the honesty of it. Some nations are indeed shitholes, perhaps more nations are than are not. Haters detest that same honesty, and see in it all of the imperial boorish arrogance of which their nation, as a superpower, is undoubtedly capable. Trump is an exaggerated human being for an exaggerated nation.

He is in every sense a thoroughly American figure, one it is impossible to imagine emerging from any other nation, and especially from the still class bound continent of Europe. Despite enormous wealth, he has the tastes, culinary and otherwise, of the American working class. He likes McDonalds and American football, he loves wealth and conspicuous display (his lift is designed like some solid gold boudoir, as if Liberace might be found in a corner playing the piano). He speaks his mind, like any good US citizen. He certainly likes women, and seemingly of a Playboy blonde haired busty stereotype too. He is the billionaire that would exist in a cartoon about billionaires, and is perhaps the Simpsons character who required least alteration to appear. And before any consideration of policy, indeed in the teeth of daring to look at what his political programme actually seems about, it is this, his quintessential Americanness, that explains the deep loathing in which he is held by US liberals.

Imagine spending your whole life learning that capitalism unjustly rewards the wrong people, and then crude Donald Trump comes along. Imagine learning that white people are responsible for all socials ills, and then this very white male who has made himself orange emerges from your fevered race based nightmares. Imagine being a Washington elite, so desperate to mimic European sophistication, a Frasier or a Niles in the diplomatic service, and along comes this blundering version of your plain speaking father. Imagine being a student Communist confronted with this ultimate Capitalist, a beta Male despising this Alpha aggressor, an Ivy League radical determined upon the rapid redistribution of all wealth except your own, a college professor of feminist studies certain that 'toxic males' have left you childless and unlovable rather than your own embittered choices.

The thinking of the US liberal on Trump, the psychology behind the hate, is not difficult to fathom. He is so hideously lowbrow, so uncultured, so disgustingly American. And he represents you on the international stage. Having been taught to despise everything about your own nation, you hardly want such a powerful symbolic representation of it in charge or representing you. You want an intersectional Muslim lesbian as your representative, not this Old White Man.

The reaction to Trump therefore speaks more to the prejudices he provokes from others than to the prejudices he holds himself. In a classic example of transference the labels quickly assigned to him-racist, sexist, bigot, authoritarian, would-be dictator-all describe his strongest opponents and the Cultural Marxist political movement he resists rather than himself. He is an impediment to the total authority over speech, thought and rule that Cultural Marxists crave, the single most evident 'fuck you' by any individual or electorate to the global dominance of Cultural Marxist ideas. He represents this resistance as both a candidate and as a person, embodying everything the Cultural Marxist detests. Unashamed patriotism? Check. National self-interest above globalist agenda? Check. Old? Check. White? Check. Male? Check. American exceptionalism given human form, endangering a determined attempt to portray America as exceptionally worthless? Check. No wonder they hate him.

It is also astonishing the extent to which hatred blinds Trump's opponents to his strengths, a reality he has been cunning and ruthless enough to repeatedly exploit. Trump thrives on being underestimated. His ego is not a hindrance, but a rocket fuel. The same applies to his ability to hold a grudge. Nothing inspired his victory more than the condescending mockery he received at the hands of men like Obama. Again and again opponents of Trump repeat these errors, mocking him and underestimating him in ways that power him to success. His supporters feel this way too, they identify with him all the more, because they are often the ignored, the neglected, the scorned. Trump had both the political intelligence and the moral decency, yes decency, to listen to these neglected Americans when nobody else did, and they love him for it. Rightly so.

For if Trump is bombastic, he has cause to be. He took a million dollar investment, a very significant head start of course, and turned it into a multi billion dollar business. He has gone bust, been virtually broke, and come back stronger. He has suffered reverses and turned them into triumphs. He has taken huge risks, some of which paid off, some of which didn't. He has perfected the art of the deal. He was the least favoured candidate in a field of equally privileged, sometimes equally wealthy but far more politically connected rivals, and he crushed them, one by one. He has endured the most sustained campaign of relentless hatred and the most dedicated efforts of internal political opposition short of actual revolution seen in US history, and he has kept on winning.

And on the international stage he is taking the mantle of leadership of the free world seriously in ways no other recent US President has dared to do. He has defended freedom at home as well as abroad, freedom of speech and thought as well as of proclaimed identity or mere self indulgence. To almost universal disregard at home, his tour of the Far East was a diplomatic triumph. In his first term he has somehow managed to fulfil campaign pledges despite running sabotage from within all political parties and from all sides. He has lowered taxes and raised GDP and created jobs. He has managed to slowly retreat from foreign wars, whilst simultaneously not retreating from global leadership, bringing dictators to the table to negotiate peace whilst offering none of the type of hideous concessions Obama offered to Iran. He has recognised the rights of Israel, despite a global, Islamic and UN led effort to make Israel a pariah State. The determination all this represents is astounding. His strengths of personality and policy far outweigh his obvious and admitted flaws.

We have also seen the war against Trump progress by the exact same stages as the war against Brexit. At first the established elite were greatly amused by this challenge to their authority and worldview. Endless hours of footage exists in which they mocked and scoffed, regarding the chances of a Trump Presidency as less than zero. They didn't just mock Trump himself, but anyone who dared to take him seriously. First they said he would never run. Then they said he would never win against established Republican contenders. Then they said he would never receive the nomination as the official Republican candidate. Then they said he would be trounced by Hilary, and were still saying it even during the vote.

Reality however has a way of intruding on Cultural Marxist dreams. It does not accord to their desires quite as easily as their penchant for demanding it should suggests. Unlike individuals in an increasingly authoritarian society, reality itself cannot be browbeaten or bullied or forced to climb down, although they will try. Enough electoral integrity remained for Trump to win, although it is likely if or when the Democrats get back in power they will swiftly move to change that (which is the purpose of their talk about fixing the electoral college system). The war began in ridicule, but continued with ruthless partisan dedication.

It began, of course, even before Trump was elected. We now know that the departing Obama administration was hard at work planting the seeds of destruction, just in case the result went wrong. They were wiretapping Trump Tower and securing semi-legal permissions to investigate members of the Trump team, Trump associates and Trump employees. They were exceptionally busy handling both these moves, ones which would have made Nixon blush, and getting their FBI bag handlers to squash any and all investigations of Hilary. They were marshalling client judges to sign off this dubious activity. Everything has to be given a veneer of legality. At around the same time the planning of the Russian collusion smear took place, organised by the Hilary campaign team, the Democratic Party as a whole, and Never Trump RINOs like the late Senator McCain. Again, we now know, thanks to the closure of the disgraceful Mueller investigation with no evidence of collusion and no real evidence of obstruction, that all of the material in the disgusting dossier and the subsequent three years of running opposition was based on an outrageous lie.

We may ask ourselves what kind of society sees a mainstream political party pay for sexual smears and charges of treasonable behaviour to be concocted against a political opponent, then sees the mainstream media all enthusiastically set off baying for blood like hounds in pursuit of Actaeon, with no come back for all of this grotesque abuse of power? Imagine what such persons can do to an ordinary citizen if this is what they can do to a Presidential candidate and a then elected President? Three years of constant lies repeated every single hour of every day in the mainstream press both in the US and internationally. The smearing of a character, the arrest and punishment of associates on totally unrelated charges, the ongoing attempt to bring down a democratically elected leader on entirely false charges. The creation of similar unproven allegations against men like Kavanaugh, throwing aside all normal judicial procedure and all established concepts regarding the need to probe allegations before treating them as truth. And have we seen anyone in our mainstream Cultural Marxist media apologise for this? Have we seen the nature of their coverage of Trump change? These people and their masters should be serving sentences for an attempted anti-democratic coup.

But once again, the key point to remember is that the war against Trump is a war against you. The ordinary voter is not to be trusted making these decisions. They can elect someone who isn't signed up to the Cultural Marxist agenda. So control of the institutions is deployed to try to reverse that. Both Trump and Brexit show just how total the Cultural Marxist control of the media is and of many branches of government regardless of election results. The anti Trump witch-hunt, all based on total fiction, very nearly succeeded. They will keep trying. Their Cultural Marxist ideology cannot compromise or pause or reflect. It can only attack.

28

Another Devil's Dictionary: Defining Cultural Marxist Tropes and Prejudices

"But if thought corrupts language, language can also corrupt thought."

—George Orwell, Politics and the English Language

As well as controlling history, Cultural Marxists always seek to control language. The assault on free speech we see in the West today is a direct consequence of Cultural Marxist control of key institutions, particularly their assumption of leading roles within the police, legal profession and judiciary. The repeated politically motivated prosecutions of people such as Tommy Robinson, the barring of people like Lauren Southern from entering or public speaking in the UK, the arrest of a man for quoting Churchill on the street or others for quoting the Bible, and even a recent case in which the British police visited the home of a man who had tweeted a limerick about transsexuals and informed that whilst he had broken no laws they were there to check on the nature of his thoughts, should collectively worry anyone aware of the role of free speech as a primary means by which the classical liberal values of the West are collectively defended.

Once again a seemingly positive cultural shift, in the form of greater politeness and consideration towards others in public speech, has been used as an excuse to move towards an increasingly totalitarian system in which certain thoughts and expressed ideas, even those with no direct link to any instance of harm, are proscribed and prosecuted, with those innocent of everything except defying Cultural Marxist attitudes risking the denial of their liberty and what amounts to arbitrary arrest and imprisonment. Once again this shift is both hypocritical and selective, with an ever increasing violence of language and behaviour allowed towards those who do not fit into Cultural Marxist victim groups.

Specific instances of this hypocrisy abound. When a group of sixteen year old Catholic schoolboys dared to wear MAGA hats recently it was almost inevitable that widespread hatred and demonization from the supposedly 'liberal' press would follow. The egregious crime of these children was to signal a different attitude to the ones Cultural Marxists have been trying to enforce on all children and adults throughout the developed world. The words 'Make America Great Again' are considered an act of violence, whereas multiple violent assaults towards people wearing these hats, also easily found in footage available on the Internet, have never occasioned criticism from mainstream media sources. Whilst wearing the MAGA hat is the surface crime, of course, the actual crime these children displayed was in being white without being ashamed of the fact or apologising for it.

When the group was approached by a Native American activist of advanced years who proceeded to beat a drum and chant slogans in their faces, whilst another group shouted racist insults towards these disturbingly white children, liberal media immediately cast the confrontation as one in which their mere presence, choice of hat and facial expressions cast them as villainous targets deserving of censure, contempt and violence. One of the children, who offered no violence in response to provocation, actually had the nerve to smile. This smile of course, in the twisted thinking of Cultural

Marxism, was an assault, an example of 'micro-aggression' and 'white privilege'. What does it say about an ideology that it considers smiling a crime, based on the skin colour of the child smiling?

Bill Meyer, typically, used his national US television platform to launch a sustained attack on these children. For smiling. For wearing a hat he doesn't like. For having the wrong skin colour. As ever, subsequent footage emerged completely contradicting the liberal assumption that the white children instigated the confrontation. As ever, this was barely noticed by Cultural Marxists who had already delivered their knee-jerk hatreds and moved on to another target. This, it should be remembered, from those who have nothing but excuses when a Cultural Marxist Antifa member hits a Trump supporter with a bicycle lock, or when leftist students riot to deny free speech, or when in an incident that curiously mirrors the one they are outraged with leftist teenage girls assaulted an elderly veteran holding a pro Trump banner.

It is in distortions of language that the thinking which allows selective violence begins. This is what Orwell so brilliantly recognised in Animal Farm ('all animals are equal but some animals are more equal than others' summarises much Cultural Marxist 'thought') and 1984. Without doublethink, without distortions of the accepted meanings of words, it is much more difficult for distortions of the accepted rules of behaviour to occur. To justify political violence, the targets must first be demonised in language, and the perpetrators of violence conditioned in language to regard their own crimes as acts of valour. This is why the Cultural Marxist assault on the established meaning of words is so significant and so disastrous in its social consequences. As an illustration of how this functions, and by homage to the example set by Ambrose Bierce in The Devil's Dictionary, I outline below some of the key terms and ideas deployed by Cultural Marxism. Each is presented in two ways, first with the meaning claimed by Cultural Marxists, and secondly with the actual meaning or practical consequence of the idea. Cultural Marxist meanings are designated CM and real meanings are designated RM.

Anti-Fascist

(CM) Stalwart defenders of decency and morality opposed to Neo Nazis, white supremacists and all manifestations of the growing problem of far right and fascist attitudes.

(RM) The type of Cultural Marxist most likely to engage in online harassment, boycotting or exclusion of anyone who isn't a Cultural Marxist, together with violent street thugs affiliated with hard left groups.

Bigotry

(CM) The small mindedness exclusive to conservatives, traditionalists, libertarians, nationalists, classical liberals, Republicans, Tories, the English, Israelis, and anyone who voices any objection to Cultural Marxism on any grounds.

(RM) The mode of rigidly narrow thought perfected by Cultural Marxists and their lack of self knowledge of that.

Diversity

(CM) The strength of our modern society. Diversity is wonderful and always to be praised. It represents the harmonious melting pot of different races and cultures building a better society together. Western cultures need to be more diverse.

(RM) The word to be used when denying any diversity of thought or in the name of which discrimination towards white people can be justified. The belief that the most diverse cultures on the planet are not diverse enough, whereas the least diverse are.

Equality

(CM) Giving everyone in society the same opportunities and chances.

(RM) Denying opportunities and chances towards white people and straight people.

Fake News

(CM) The sort of manipulative propaganda deployed by Trump, by Leave voters, and by fascists. Denials of science and weird conspiracy theories.

(RM) Any news not controlled by Cultural Marxists and not pushing a Cultural Marxist agenda. Anything remotely balanced written about Trump, Brexit or white people. Any scientific fact or rational evidence that contradicts Cultural Marxism.

Fascist

(CM) A far right wing person. There are more and more fascists around and anyone who isn't a Cultural Marxist can be one. Fascists need to be opposed and destroyed.

(RM) A specific Italian political ideology only widely prevalent in the early 20th century, created by former Communists. Also anyone who isn't a Cultural Marxist who wins a debate against them.

Gammon

(CM) An ignorant or stupid person, a racist or a fool.

(RM) A term of racist abuse popular with Cultural Marxists.

Gender

(CM) An identity we choose which has nothing to do with biology.

(RM) An identity we are born with which has everything to do with biology.

Homophobia

(CM) The inherent tendency of straight people to discriminate against and oppress homosexuals. It is rife in western society.

(RM) A word that is useful when one wishes to discriminate against and oppress heterosexuals. In its CM meaning, actually rife in non western societies.

Imperialism

(CM) The disgusting history of the West in enslaving, oppressing and killing non whites and stealing their land.

(RM) The historical period in which western nation states were especially successful. The period in which western nations were not being enslaved and oppressed by non whites. A word which excuses hatred and prejudice towards western nation states, their people, and their history.

Inclusion

(CM) Making society fairer for non whites and minority groups by including them.

(RM) Excluding white people.

Islamophobia

(CM) The unreasoning prejudice and hatred towards Islam displayed by racists, bigots and far right scum.

(RM) Any rational objection to fourteen centuries of evil.

Misogyny

(CM) The unreasoning hatred and prejudice towards women rife in western culture.

(RM) The unreasoning hatred and prejudice towards women rife in non western cultures.

Nationalism

(CM) A stupid, irrational and prejudiced devotion to the illusory superiority of one's own nation or people. Nationalism is common to the ignorant and stupid and stands in the way of global happiness and progress. Nationalism created Nazism and the horrors of two world wars. Only when we evolve beyond it will human beings live in peace and harmony.

(RM) Any normal feeling of affection or loyalty towards the place where you were born, the land where you live, or the people who share your language, culture and history. Nationalism has been common throughout human history as long as nations have existed and has inspired some of the greatest thinkers and artists in history. Nationalists defeated Nazism and nationalists made tremendous sacrifices to end two world wars.

Non Binary

(CM) A person who refuses to be defined by other's expectations of their gender.

(RM) A person who insists that others agree with their delusions regarding gender.

Progressive

(CM) A person who holds the enlightened views and values which improve society.

(RM) A person who holds the Cultural Marxist views and values that are destroying western civilisation.

Racism

(CM) The unthinking hatred and prejudice based on race that has shaped western civilisation. Racism only exists with power, so it is exclusively something which white people inflict on non white people.

(RM) Any hatred based on race, such as the detestation of white people held by Cultural Marxists. Power just makes it easier to enact but anyone can be racist and all cultures and races have been both victims and perpetrators of it. Western civilisation possesses the least racist cultures on the planet.

Religion of Peace

(CM) Islam.

(RM) Any religion other than Islam.

Social Justice

(CM) Measures to increase fairness by tackling discrimination, racism and prejudice in society.

(RM) Legislative and social engineering measures to make society more discriminatory, racist and prejudiced.

Straight

(CM) The sexual orientation that has oppressed and demonised all others.

(RM) The sexual orientation that is currently being oppressed and demonised.

Toxic Masculinity

(CM) The tendency in male identity towards violence, harm and mistreatment of others. A natural propensity to evil unique to males.

(RM) A useful means of ridiculing, belittling and demonising anyone who happens to be male.

Transphobia

(CM) The fear and prejudice suffered by the trans community.

(RM) Criticising people for not being transsexuals or not wanting to have sex with transsexuals.

Virtue

(CM) Possessing enlightened qualities, following enlightened principles or being Woke.

(RM) Telling everyone on Facebook how Woke you are. Virtue has no reference to actual behaviour in a traditional moral sense.

White Privilege

(CM) The inherent advantages white people gain by advantage of their skin colour, their unawareness of this, and the conspiratorial ways they use this to achieve and maintain power over non whites.

(RM) A race hate theory.

Whiteness

(CM) An illusory set of qualities white people have created as a social construct in order to oppress others.

(RM) The colour and race Cultural Marxists think it is enlightened to hate.

Woke

(CM) Being aware of your advantages as a white person, as a male, or as a straight person and trying to be fair and decent to others.

(RM) Fully accepting Cultural Marxist bullshit without possessing the critical awareness or historical knowledge that challenges these obvious absurdities.

Xenophobia

(CM) The hatred of others and of different races and cultures common to the ignorant, the stupid and to fascists and bigots.

(RM) Not hating your own country.

29

AFTERWORD:
TOPICS NOT COVERED

THIS IS A LENGTHY BUT BY NO MEANS EXHAUSTIVE analysis of the nature of both Western Civilisation and the Cultural Marxism that threatens it. I hope it has made clear two main ideas, firstly that western civilisation has created a great deal of good that deserves a better defence than it currently receives, and secondly that Cultural Marxist attitudes can only lead towards greater disunity and disruption within the West even if they do not lead to its complete collapse. The promise of a better society which Cultural Marxism holds out is as dishonest and dangerous as the similar promises made by religious fundamentalism or by Communism in the 20th century. It is the great tragedy of our times, perhaps, that so many people are now convinced that they are doing good whilst they busily enact or support evil.

We have already seen the consequences. Thousands of children raped in the UK, with little official response save to try to silence working class voices of protest. Free speech threatened in western nations to the greatest degree seen in centuries. Effective blasphemy laws enacted against critics of Islam. Basic principles of democracy, once commonly understood and so widely supported that most of the populace were prepared to risk death to defend them, now denied or reversed.

When it comes to issues like mass immigration, even the most cursory familiarity with actual experience, with the kind of working class experience few middle and upper class Cultural Marxists ever possess themselves, quickly reveals the sheer abject stupidity of Cultural Marxist ideas. Those of us who have lived in areas blighted by high crime and social alienation consequent upon untrammelled levels of immigration know that the support of open borders common to Cultural Marxists is a selfish and perverse indulgence, based on an entirely inaccurate assumption that other cultures are either equal or superior to ours. The naivety of many of the views spread by Cultural Marxists is often based on a complete historical ignorance deliberately fostered by ideologues of a previous generation.

For some these beliefs would be endearing if their consequences were not so tragic. The idea of a sort of Gene Rodenberry future, a future in which all races and peoples are united as human beings and equally good, is attractive. But it is not the reality we live. There are cultures where the rape of children is a social norm. Several immigrant rapists have themselves pointed this fact out in court. But still we do not listen. There are cultures in which, having suffered devastating civil wars or still enacting ancient ethnic or religious schisms, the lessons of conflict have brutalised human sensibilities. Immigration from such places is inherently dangerous to the wellbeing of the societies they move into. We have seen this with various Eastern hatreds playing themselves out in Western streets. We see it in the growth of antisemitism again in the West, fuelled by Islamic communities and the leftist alliance with them.

There are topics related to all this I have not covered, but which I might include in a latter edition or separate work. The Cultural Marxist attitudes to the US and the US working class has been mentioned in passing, but not expounded at length, but there is a remarkable similarity with how that operates and how Cultural Marxists view Britain. The Cultural Marxist hatred of Israel has not been treated to a separate chapter, nor has my own belief that Jewish patriots are natural allies of conservatives and traditionalists.

There are also more positive global reactions that offer some hope for the future, usually by the degree to which they are despised by the mainstream media. Trump was elected, despite the most corrupt abuses of power from the departing Obama administration. Trump is still there, despite the recently concluded shameful disgrace of the Mueller witchhunt. The growth of populist movements across Europe fighting back against Cultural Marxism, particularly in Italy, Hungary, Poland and France is hugely encouraging for anyone who values either any specific western national identity or western civilisation and freedom as a whole. In Italy we see a particularly fascinating and hopeful alliance between a populist Right and a populist Left (between Matteo Salvini's League and Luigi Di Maio's Five Star Movement). It is this kind of willingness of populists, who are simply those capable of hearing what the People actually want, that offers the best hope of saving any part of western civilisation from the utter ruination, moral and economic, which following Cultural Marxism offers.

The utopian promise of Cultural Marxism, this mythical belief that we already inhabit a world where all cultures are equal and only have to 'wake' to love and respect for others to own it today, is a suicide pill presented as an enticing chocolate. We face the choice as a culture of being hardheaded rationalists or ideologically warped utopians, of relying on logic and evidence or relying on emotion and virtue signalling hysteria. In a recent street confrontation an SJW opined that emotions are more real than facts. This was really only an unusually honest moment in a culture where delusion is being lauded as progress.

The areas in western civilisation where Cultural Marxist attitudes face greater resistance than they do in the UK or US are areas which for historic reasons have a far more recent experience of real tyranny or a far more sustained experience of real external threat. Eastern Europeans do not feel the self hatred and need to apologise that Western Europeans do. They also know that leftist pieties can very easily lead to secret police torture cells and mounds of slaughtered innocents. Similarly in places like Hungary and Poland, so often through their history conquered and reconquered and so often engaged in the active defence of Christendom against the advance of Islam, the idea that Islam is a religion of peace, that there is nothing unique or worth preserving about western nations and western freedom, fools far fewer people. I have not discussed these places in separate chapters, but it is by following their example that we will regain our own sense of pride and worth.

It is a very sad thing to be an Englishman, an inheritor of one of the proudest histories of courage and innovation and moral rectitude across the globe, and to live amongst so many who hate and despise and misunderstand almost all of that history. But there have been many times before when the story of England seemed to have ended. The British and Anglo-Saxon thread of resistance which can be traced from Boudicca to King Arthur to Alfred the Great, and which runs through our national island story from the sighting of the fleets of Caesar to those of Philip II of Spain or to the squadrons of the Luftwaffe only seventy years ago, is another aspect of western civilisation which has informed this book without being separately discussed within it. But this spirit of dogged resistance and eccentric individualism, so central to British character, must be understood to have any understanding of events like the Brexit vote, which if it did anything at all provided proof that the British people still love liberty, even if British politicians do not.

And for those aware of the true extent of Western Civilisation and our inheritance of it, our birthright, such contemporary political rebellions also hark back, ultimately, to the founding myths of western identity, to the Roman Horatius (Publius Horatius Cocles) defending the bridge, or to Greek Spartans resisting Persian autocracy. There are many ways to cry 'freedom', including by a vote. Today we who remember our past, we who love western civilisation, must also ask our enemies, "who amongst you is brave enough to face a Roman soldier". We must rediscover that pride, or die.